THE

PRAYER-GAUGE DEBATE.

BY

PROF. TYNDALL, FRANCIS GALTON,
AND OTHERS,

AGAINST

DR. LITTLEDALE, PRESIDENT McCOSH,
THE DUKE OF ARGYLL, CANON LYDDON, AND
"THE SPECTATOR."

BOSTON:
CONGREGATIONAL PUBLISHING SOCIETY,
BEACON STREET.
1876.

BOSTON:
STEREOTYPED BY C. J. PETERS AND SON,
73 FEDERAL STREET.

Press of Rand, Avery, & Co.

INTRODUCTORY.

In the month of July, 1872, "The London Contemporary Review" published a paper, entitled "The Prayer for the Sick: Hints towards a Serious Attempt to estimate its Value." Prof. John Tyndall fathered it with an Introduction, while disavowing the authorship. His name, and not any intrinsic novelty or merit in the thing itself, gave significance and notoriety to it.

The succeeding numbers of The Review contained replies, which were followed by rejoinders from Prof. Tyndall and his disguise. Other magazines entered the lists. Francis Galton marshalled the doughty columns of statistical tables, to support Mr. Tyndall, in "The Fortnightly Review." For weeks the great newspapers of London were loaded with editorials upon the Prayer-Gauge, and with communications prepared by all classes and conditions of men, from a bookseller's clerk to the highest dignitaries of the English Church and peers of the realm. The Prayer-Gauge Debate was the sensation of the season.

The question in dispute was not the question of a season, however, but of all time. The objections to the efficacy of prayer were none of them new, and never will be old. They have come up afresh with every sun-rising since Cain disputed with Abel; and they will continue to come up till the millennium. It is well for Christian believers to examine them: it is an advantage to look at them in the flaming light in which scientific unbelievers delight to exhibit them. It will assist in establishing the truth to put the objections in their strongest array, face to face with the answers which the Christian intelligence of the day has given.

Those who followed the discussion at the time in "The Contemporary Review," "Fortnightly Review," and "The Spectator," will welcome a volume containing, in orderly arrangement, all the articles which touched the substance of the dispute; while the greater number who have not seen the English publications, and know them only by hearsay, will be glad to read and weigh these papers for themselves. They are worth preserving; for they exhibit principles and methods of reasoning of permanent value.

We reprint, in the order in which they appeared, the articles from the two reviews, for and against this Christian doctrine, with editorials from "The Spectator," and selections from the communications of correspondents. Of course, we assume no responsibility as to the substance or expression of the arguments on either side.

JOHN O. MEANS.

CONTENTS.

I.

THE "PRAYER FOR THE SICK."

HINTS TOWARDS A SERIOUS ATTEMPT TO ESTIMATE ITS VALUE.

THIS is the title of the paper which started this discussion in "The Contemporary Review," seventh year, new series, the number for July, 1872, pp. 205-210.

Strahan & Co. are the publishers, 56 Ludgate Hill, London.

The authorship, distinctly disavowed by Mr. Tyndall, is generally attributed to Sir Henry Thompson, F. R. C. S., an eminent London surgeon, professor of surgery U. Coll. Hospital, &c., author of several important medical works.

I.

THE "PRAYER FOR THE SICK."

HINTS TOWARDS A SERIOUS ATTEMPT TO ESTIMATE ITS VALUE.

THE following suggestive letter has been placed in my hands, with a view to publication. It is sure, I think, to interest the thoughtful readers of "The Contemporary Review." It deals, indeed, with a subject which interests everybody, and regarding which all manner of men, from the prime-minister downwards, have given the public the benefit of their views.

If such be attainable, it is surely desirable to have clearer notions than we now possess of the action of "Providence" in physical affairs. Two opposing parties here confront each other, — the one affirming the habitual intrusion of supernatural power in answer to the petitions of men; the other questioning, if not denying, any such intrusion. The writer of the letter wishes to bring these opposing affirmations to an experimental test. He considers the subject to be accessible to experiment, and makes a proposal, which, if faithfully carried out, would, he thinks, displace assertion by demonstration as regards the momentous point in question.

It was justly stated by the Archbishop of York at a recent meeting of the supporters of the Palestine Exploration Fund, that the progress of the human mind is from vagueness towards precision. The letter before us seems an illustration of this tendency. Instead of leaving the subject to the random assertions of half-informed sceptics on the one hand, and hazy lecturers of the Victoria Institute on the other, the writer seeks to confer quantitative precision on the action of the supernatural in Nature. His proposal is so fair, and his mode of stating it so able and conciliatory, that I could not, when asked to do so, refuse to give it the support implied by these few lines of introduction.

John Tyndall.

Athenæum Club, June, 1872.

Dear Professor Tyndall,

SINCE our conversation the other night, when you were good enough to listen to a suggestion I made relative to a means of determining the value of prayer to the Deity, it occurred to me to put the idea into writing, and to ask you to do me the further kindness of looking at it in this shape.

It seems to me impossible, at the present day, to find ourselves in contact with a source of power available for human ends (or affirmed to be so on high authority), without recognizing a necessity, or even that it is a duty, to estimate its value. And especially if the power be one which is effective for the production of physical results, is it desirable to examine its nature, and to measure its extent, and the conditions under which it works.

The value of prayer to the Deity has been recognized in all ages and by all nations, not merely by the ignorant and superstitious, but by the more cultivated portions of the human race; and I think it may be said, that, among the great body of religious people of all denominations in this country, a belief in its efficacy is almost universally professed. As to the objects which it is believed are attainable by prayer, they are almost without limit as to kind. Taking as an authority that well-known compendium, which none will dispute to be the national epitome of English religious idea on the subject, "The Book of Common Prayer,"[1] the legitimate objects of supplication to God may be classified as follows: —

Class A. Spiritual improvement, moral superiority, intellectual power.

[1] Although not used by Dissenters, they do not reject it on account of its contents, since its very phraseology is often employed by them, but, for the most part, because all *forms* are deemed by them undesirable.

Class B. National supremacy; preservation from pestilence, famine, and battles; the fertility of the soil, whether suitable for the growth and preservation of vegetable products; the health, wealth, and long life of the chief national ruler; a special share of grace and wisdom for the nobility, and for members of the legislature and of the Executive.

Class C. For all that are in danger; for the preservation of travellers, of sick persons, of young children, prisoners, orphans, and widows; protection against murder and sudden death.

Class D. Comprehends *special* forms for occasional use; *e.g.*, for "moderate rain and showers," &c; that "scarcity and dearth may be turned into cheapness and plenty;" that "this plague and grievous sickness may be withdrawn;" and the prayer for "sick persons," which is not precise in its requests on their behalf.

From all the foregoing, it is impossible to resist the conclusion, already more than hinted, that a very ample belief exists in the Christian Church in the efficacy of prayer to God to avert dire physical evils, which without it might occur; such, for example, as disease and death. Were any one, however, hardy enough to question this, it would suffice to point out that the custom of offering prayers for the recovery of sick persons when in great danger is almost universal here. And it may be added, that, in the larger and more ancient section of the Church, prayer still continues on behalf of the deceased, — a custom, perhaps, not less pious and reasonable than the first-named.

Now, I propose to examine this subject from one point of view only, in the endeavor to discover a means of demonstrating, in some tangible form, the efficacy of prayer. I commence by remarking, however, that the objects of prayer in Class *A* clearly present inordinate difficulties, and are obviously unfitted for our purpose. Class *B* furnishes subjects which might be examined, but which are less easy of treatment than some of those to be found in Classes *C* and *D*. But, even here, elements of disturbance present themselves; thus, in reference to the influence of prayer on states of the weather in limited localities, that food may be cheapened, that travellers may be preserved from accident, &c., it is certain that considerable difficulty would arise in any systematic attempt to arrive at accurate conclusions. But this leads me to remark, that there appears to be one source from a study of which the absolute calculable value of prayer (I speak with the utmost reverence) can almost certainly be ascertained. I mean its influence in affecting the course of a malady, or in averting the fatal termination. For it must be admitted that such an important influence, manifestly either does, or does not exist. If it does, a careful investigation of diseased persons by good pathologists, working with this end seriously in view, must determine the fact. The fact determined, it is simply a matter of further careful clinical observation to estimate the extent or degree in which prayer is effective. And the next step would be to consider how far it is practicable to extend this benefit among the sick and dying. And I can conceive few inquiries which are more pregnant with good to humanity when this stage has been arrived at.

You will naturally next say, What practical shape does the method take by which you propose to attain your end? The method has its difficulties; but I see none that are insuperable. If I may reckon on the active co-operation of those who most believe in the value of such prayer (and I think I have a right to do so), the inquiry will be easy; for few more interesting subjects of inquiry can exist for the honest believer than the extent of man's influence with Heaven at the most momentous crisis in his personal history.

Before entering on the details demanded, it is first necessary to remark, that prayer for the recovery of sick persons exists in two distinct forms, or, if I may use the term, in two orders or degrees of quality. For, first, there are the general prayers for the sick, made, without distinction as to individuals or to numbers, on most occasions of public worship. These prayers are offered by, perhaps, thirty thousand congregations every Sunday in our country, since it is no less the practice of the Dissenter than of the Churchman to remember devoutly the sick in the weekly supplication. But, besides these, there are the special prayers for individual sick persons, which are, by general consent, deemed also necessary; and thus it is, that, when the patient holds a very high place in society, a special form of petition is sometimes ordained to be used throughout the national churches for his recovery. It is one of the advantages of rank and gentle birth in England, that special prayers are made for such, every week at least, in most churches throughout the country.

The first kind, or "general prayer," then, must be held to have a certain value not inconsiderable, since it is this kind which is relied on against the dangers of travel, of murder, and of sudden death, and respecting which no other or special petitions are provided. This general prayer for the recovery from sickness is constantly ascending, if I may use the term, in a broad stream to Heaven; yet, its objects ("all men") being so numerous, it is not held to suffice for all individual cases: hence the second kind, or special prayer. And the object sought by those who are interested in the recovery of the sick, obviously is to concentrate the special prayers of many on the recovery of one, in the belief, that, by this means, the malady may be more certainly checked than were the patient's fate to depend only on the influence of the "general prayer." With this end it is, that the special prayers of a congregation are asked for A or B, or a special prayer-meeting is held to offer the one object of petition. I have been myself present at such meetings, and have witnessed the number, the minuteness, and the length of the petitions.

Now, the latter kind, or "special prayer," is that which readily lends itself to the earnest inquirer in this matter; and it is by its means, if carefully and conscientiously pursued, that we may certainly arrive, if at all, at a solution of the great question I have proposed.

The following appears to me to indicate the manner of conducting the inquiry. It should be pursued on a system somewhat analogous to that which is pursued by the faculty when a question arises as to the value of any particular mode of treating disease. For example, a new remedy has been proposed, or is said on high authority to be efficacious; and as authority does not suffice in medicine, further than to recommend a given course, and never to prescribe it, the remedy is carefully tested. Usually a hospital or a ward is assigned for the purpose. All the patients suffering from the disease to be treated are, during a certain period, divided into two classes; and all are subjected, as far as possible, to the same conditions, that single one of treatment alone excepted. The ages, sexes, and many other particulars of the patients, are taken into account, and duly noted. The one class is treated by the old system; and the other, by the new remedy. When a very large number — for in large numbers only is there truth — has been thus dealt with, the results are compared, and the value of the remedy can be definitely expressed; that is, its influence above or below that of the old treatment, as the case may be, will appear in the percentage of recovery, or of other results.

Now, after much thought and examination of the various questions and objections which may possibly be urged, I do not hesitate to propose an analogous arrangement, in order to estimate and rightly appreciate the influence of special prayer to check disease, or to avert death.

We possess unquestionable data in reference to certain well-known maladies, particularly the fevers of eruptive type; such as small-pox, typhoid, scarlet fever, &c. Of some local acute disorders, such as pneumonia, we know what is termed the natural history pretty well, — their duration, and probable termination, at different ages, &c. The mortality which follows the great surgical operations at different ages is a matter known and determined; for example, after lithotomy and lithotrity, amputations of the limbs, hernia, &c. The very large records of past cases which exist, and the very wide and careful researches which have been made, have had for their result the production of known numerical mortality-rates per cent, and applicable to future patients of different ages and conditions. Indeed, the whole system of life-assurance is, all the world over, based solely on the accuracy of such data, and on the certainty with which they will reproduce themselves. Whatever these numerical results have been, — whether the mortality-rates deduced belong to healthy lives or to diseased lives — all have been necessarily made subject to the conditions of human life as it now exists, and including, among a thousand other influences, that most important one of "general prayer" by the whole Christian Church for "all men," as it has been already described, and influencing as it does, whatever may be its extent, the sick, the suffering, those exposed to murder and sudden death, &c., throughout the whole world. Subject to this influence is that of every drug prescribed. Influenced by this is the result of every surgical operation.

Now, for the purpose of our inquiry, I do not propose to ask that one single child of man should be deprived of his participation in all that belongs to him of this vast influence. But I ask that one single ward, or hospital, under the care of first-rate physicians and surgeons, containing certain numbers of patients afflicted with those diseases which have been best studied, and of which the mortality-rates are best known, — whether the diseases are those which are treated by medical or by surgical remedies, — should be, during a period of not less, say, than three or five years, made the object of special prayer by the whole body of the faithful, and that, at the end of that time, the mortality-rates should be compared with the past rates, and also with that of other leading hospitals similarly well managed during the same period. Granting that time is given, and numbers are sufficiently large, so as to insure a minimum of error from accidental disturbing causes, the experiment will be exhaustive and complete.

I might have proposed to treat two sides of the same hospital, managed by the same men; one side to be the object of special prayer, the other to be exempted from all prayer. It would have been the most rigidly logical and philosophical method. But I shrink from depriving any of — I had almost said — his natural inheritance in the prayers of Christendom. Practically, too, it would have been impossible. The unprayed-for ward would have attracted the prayers of believers, as surely as the lofty tower attracts electric fluid. The experiment would be frustrated. But the opposite character of my proposal will commend it to those who are naturally the most interested in its success, — those, namely, who conscientiously and devoutly believe in the efficiency, against disease and death, of special prayer. I open a field for the exercise of their devotion. I offer an occasion of demonstrating to the faithless an imperishable record of the real power of prayer.

Athenæum Club, Pall Mall, June, 1872.

II.

"THE SPECTATOR" ON THE PROPOSED PRAYER-GAUGE.

THE earliest reply to the challenge of Mr. Tyndall and his friend appeared as an editorial in "The Spectator," July 6, 1872, No. 2,297, pp. 846, 847.

"The Spectator" is issued every Saturday, and is now approaching its fiftieth year. It is supposed to represent the best culture of the Broad Churchmen. Mr. R. H. Hutton was the editor, or one of the editors. This is numbered 1.

In the number of the succeeding week, July 13, No. 2,298, p. 879, a correspondent, with the signature A. A., follows up the editorial, opening the letter-bag of contributions to the discussion. This communication is numbered 2.

II.

THE PROPOSED PRAYER-GAUGE.

1.

PROF. TYNDALL should hardly have given the sanction of his deservedly respected name to the unworthy piece of literary irony, — for such we unhesitatingly deem it, — in which an anonymous writer in "The Contemporary Review" proposes gravely to the believers in prayer to make an attempt at quantitative measurement of God's accessibility to prayer, *i.e.*, at a physical determination of the value of special providences. If the physicists are as accurate as they are apt to be arrogant, they should at least know how to respect the religious feelings of the believers they despise, and not attempt to poke fun at them in the shape of thinly-veiled scoffs at their most profound and intimate faiths. We are aware, indeed, that some of the readers of this elaborate sarcasm have attributed it to a believer, and not a disbeliever, in the power of prayer. We will give, in a moment, our reasons for feeling confident that this is impossible; but a single sentence of the paper to which Prof. Tyndall has lent his sanction will, probably, suffice to convince most of our readers of its true nature. Speaking of the special prayers for sick people in imminent danger, the writer says, "It is one of the advantages of rank and gentle birth in England, that special prayers are made for such, every week at least, in most churches throughout the country." Few will doubt that the author has here been unable to repress the sneer of which his whole paper is an elaborate embodiment, nor that his democratic bias in this case combined for the moment with his sceptical feeling to sharpen the sting of his sentence; yet, as a matter of fact, we imagine the truth to be quite otherwise. In most churches, one hears prayers for the sick poor every Sunday; while the reserve of the rich usually prevents their asking the prayers of the congregation, even where they are not sceptical as to their value. What Mr. Tyndall's friend affects to wish is this, — that special prayers should be continually offered by all the believers in prayer who will consent to join, during three or five years, for the recovery of the patients of a single hospital, without depriving "one single child of man" of what the writer "had almost called his natural inheritance in the prayers of Christendom." He would then compare the average duration of sickness, and the average rates of mortality, in that hospital, with the same rates, for the same class of diseases, in other not specially distinguished hospitals, and regard the shortening of the average time of sickness, if any, and the diminution of the death-rate, if any, as a residuary phenomenon due to the special prayer-power concentrated on that institution. We describe this ironical proposal with something of reluctance and disgust; for we confess that we do not think subjects of this kind suitable for efforts of literary sarcasm. If sceptics like to state their doubts and their pity for others' unreasonable faith openly, we have nothing but approval to express. So, and so only, can the doubters come to understand the believers; and the believers, the doubters. But the instinct of the trapper, and the policy of the ambuscade, cannot be applied to subjects of this kind without indefinitely increasing the estrangements and bitter alienations of our religious and irreligious worlds.

And now we will justify the line we have taken about this insidious challenge, by stating why the author's proposal seems to us, what a certain number of simple religious people will very likely not find it, a covert sneer, and not the frank challenge of a cultivated inquirer. What Christians believe, for the most part, is, that God answers, sometimes in one way and sometimes in another, those prayers which really come from the depth of the heart, — prayers which cannot but be accompanied by a deep effort of submission to his higher will; and, when we say that he answers them, we mean that he makes a real answer, — whether in the way of pitiful denial, or tender assent, or assent in some different and deeper sense than that of the request itself, — which is manifest to the heart of him who offered the prayer. But we should be much surprised to learn that any man who had really given up his mind to thoughts of this kind at all had ever regarded his prayer as a sort of petty dictation to God, the effect of which might be measured, like a constituent's pressure on his representative in parliament, by the influence it exerted on the issue. You pray, if you pray in the spirit of Christ at all, not for a specific external end, but because it is a deep relief to pour out your heart to God in the frankest way possible to limited human nature, and in the hope, that, if your *wish* is not granted, your *want* may be. Suppose you pray for the recovery of a mortally sick friend, who dies. What your prayer really consists of is the confession of the blank you fear for yourself, and still more, perhaps, for others; of your dread of losing the moral help and sympathy so essential to you; of the yearning that this trouble may not come on those whom it threatens. And is not that prayer as much answered by the substitution of other and possibly more potent moral influences for those which are lost, as by the recovery of the threatened life itself? Yet "answer to prayer," in the sense of the "conciliatory" writer in "The Contemporary," as Prof. Tyndall flatteringly terms him, could mean but one thing, — that the specific life threatened should be restored.

But, beyond this, the proposal of Prof. Tyndall's friend is of a very ambiguous character, for a deeper reason. He respectfully declines to attempt applying what he calls "the more rigidly logical and philosophical method" of comparing one ward in a hospital where the inmates had every care and help, except intercessory prayer, with another, where they had all these influences, and the advantage of intercessory prayer as well; because, as he justly remarks, it would not be possible to keep religious people from offering up special prayers for the ward on which the experiment of no prayer ought to be tried. In other words, we suppose he thinks it would be difficult to discover a spiritual equivalent for the process known as hermetically sealing a glass tube against the intrusion of any physical influence from without. He is obliged, therefore, to have recourse to the inductive method known as that of "variations," rather than that of "differences." He cannot wholly deduct the influence of prayer in any case; but he suggests that a special excess of its influence might be secured in a particular case, and that you might, in this way, secure an increase of the effect in proportion to the increase of the cause, if the cause be a *vera causa* at all. But he quite forgets, that to have the true antecedent he wants, in any sense in which most Christians admit its efficacy, you must have for your antecedent a prayer that is the single expression of the heart, and not something, which, while it seems to ask one thing, is really pointed at another, and which makes the recovery of the patients in a particular hospital a mere indirect mode of applying a barometric gauge to the special providence of God. When an intimate friend asks a favor, not because he simply wants the thing he asks for, but wants to test his influence with the person whom he is soliciting, we all know that the whole condition of the request is changed, and that, very often, what the friend solicited would accede to in the former case, he would refuse as a deliberate abuse of personal influence in the latter case. No doubt, Prof. Tyndall's friend might reply, that in the Old Testament, at least, we have instances (notably Elijah's) where prayer was professedly an invitation to God to give the world some means of judging of the influence which a particular person had with him, as a kind of sign that this person was really inspired by an omnipotent and omniscient Being. But, whatever we may say of Elijah's proceeding, Christians are accustomed to think that they are forbidden to ask for signs as measures of their influence with God; and that it is to this morbid tendency that our Lord's words, even as to his own similar temptation, "Thou shalt not tempt the Lord thy God," specially apply. Certainly there is something simply revolting to the spirit of Christian prayer in the proposal to gauge indirectly, by continuous prayer for a particular institution's success, the divine susceptibility to prayer. How should we think of any one who prayed — *i.e.*, who ought to be pouring out the deepest longings of his soul — for the restoration of certain persons to health, only to make a delicate experiment on the relation between the spiritual and physical forces of the universe? Does it follow, because, in some sense, God answers true prayer, he would answer the demand for a scientifically scaled prayer-gauge? Even Elijah put his prayer for a sign openly. He asked for nothing desirable in itself, but solely for a physical sign that his God held the elements in his hands. But what Prof. Tyndall's friend desires, is, that we shall cloak our request for a sign under a request for something which we suppose to be intrinsically desirable; that we shall approach God disguised, with a sort of excuse on our lips, our object not being in itself the recovery of the patients of the particular institution, but the scientific determination of our moral command of the fountains of divine mercy. Can it be well conceived that such a proposal could be made, except in profound irony?

But Prof. Tyndall and his friend will reply, "Well, then, you confess that the power of prayer is — for physical purposes at all events — practically incalculable, since you resist, even with scorn, all attempts to test its limits; and how can you expect physicists to believe in any physical cause whatever, which is admitted to have only incalculable effects?" To which we should simply rejoin, "How, indeed? But who ever thought before of convincing physicists, as physicists, of the reality of a power, which, by the very nature of the case, they could not as physicists appeal to, even if they were convinced of its existence?" A great ambition often produces a great career; but you cannot produce a great ambition by dwelling on the charms of a great career. A great love defies death; but you cannot get a great love simply by wishing for a force strong enough to defy death. So earnest prayer may have a mysterious power which it is quite impossible to trace, even over physical events; but you cannot get earnest prayer simply from the intense desire to mould physical events to your will. Prayer is, if it is any thing at all, communion with God; and the very conditions of the case exclude this base experiment on the possible construction of a prayer-gauge. And free communion with God excludes, and necessarily excludes, the desire to dictate the answer. Its language is accommodated to the language of Isaiah, "My thoughts are not your thoughts, neither are your ways my ways, saith the Lord. For as the heavens are higher than the earth, so are my ways higher than your ways, and my thoughts than your thoughts." If Christians are not ashamed to pray sometimes for specific physical blessings, it is or ought to be, rather as the simplest expression of their anxieties, than as expecting that the divine response either must or ought to be the giving of the exact blessing, or the warding-off the exact trouble, which they name. We believe prayer to be a true power, — a power which alters the external course of the world, as well as its internal course; but we believe it on precisely the same kind of evidence on which every sane man believes that the passionate desires of individuals so often realize themselves, and that the hopes of multitudes create the great historic changes for which they cry. It seems to us far simpler to believe that those results take place through the providence of God than that they come to pass through the magic influence of human passion, — far simpler, because there are so many objects of desire which intense desire only throws into the greater distance, while with high moral and spiritual objects of desire, at all events, this is never so. But we should be as sincerely disgusted with such an experiment on God as Prof. Tyndall's friend suggests, as he is probably delighted with himself for the invention of that triumphant dilemma, into which, as he imagines, he has wedged the superstitious crowd whom he desires to expose.

2.

[TO THE EDITOR OF THE "SPECTATOR."]

SIR, — Although I agree with you in holding the letter in "The Contemporary Review" to be "an elaborate sarcasm," I still think there is one moral to be drawn from it, which, in your admirable article, you did not pause to draw; namely, the fresh testimony it affords of the utter inability of a certain class of scientific minds to understand who and what the Deity is whom Christians confess and adore. The writer practically says this: "You Christians believe that there is a certain mighty force, which you are allowed to summon at command. One person can set it in motion slightly: a large number, acting simultaneously, can move it still more. If you can secure the co-operation of a larger body still, there is no knowing what the results may not be." The writer's argument, in short, is intended as a *reductio ad absurdum* of what he conceives to be the Christian ideas of God, and men's access to him by prayer.

The striking and most melancholy feature of the letter is, that it wholly ignores the existence of any moral or even *reasonable* qualities in the Being to whom prayer is addressed. The writer has not even attained to the conception of God as a wise and good *man*, or he would never have proposed a mode of address to him, which a man of the most moderate degree of sense and decency would instinctively resent, if paid to himself. What would the writer have said to his own children, if he heard them concocting a plan for making an experiment upon his good-nature, not dictated by their real necessities or honest desires, but by curiosity as to the amount of pressure he could succeed in resisting? And, if there be a God at all, is he not likely to be at least as jealous of the moral well-being of those whom he calls his children as even the proposer of this monstrous experiment?

The writer chooses to assume as the God of the Bible a being whose relations to his creatures are not those of a moral being at all. The charge which Christ brought against the Gentiles, that they thought they would be heard for their much speaking, is here brought, for the purpose of the writer's argument, against the God whom Christ was laboring to reveal. Christ taught expressly that God regarded the sincerity of the worshipper as the first condition of his answering the prayer. The writer before us deliberately assumes that the God of the Christian's worship not only will, but is bound to, grant any petition, though dictated by the idlest curiosity, or (worse still) by the insane expectation that he will be deceived as to the real purpose for which it is presented. Surely, nothing but a virulent hostility to the religion of Christians could so blind a man to the first conditions of the problem which he is aiming to solve. I am, sir, &c., A. A.

III.

THE RATIONALE OF PRAYER.

BY THE REV. RICHARD FREDERICK LITTLEDALE, D.C.L.

THIS appeared in the August number of "The Contemporary Review," pp. 430-454, next after the number in which the question was stated. Dr. Littledale is considered an extreme Ritualist, and one of the ablest men of this section of the English Church. His contribution to the discussion may be appreciated by those who have no sympathy with his advocacy of prayers for the dead, or with his flings at Calvinism.

III.

THE RATIONALE OF PRAYER.

"For Nym, he hath heard that men of few words are the best men; and therefore he scorns to say his prayers, lest a' should be thought a coward."—SHAKSPEARE.

IN the July number of this "Review" appeared a communication from Prof. Tyndall, accompanying an unsigned letter, wherein a proposal was broached for testing the efficacy of prayer by means of inductive experiment and quantitative analysis.

Lest any readers of this paper should have omitted to examine Prof. Tyndall's contribution, it is well to say that the scheme suggested was to set apart one ward of some hospital for the reception of a number of cases of diseases, which have been satisfactorily tabulated as to the ratio of seizures and deaths; to have this ward, while under exactly the same medical treatment as the others, specially interceded for by a general union for prayer; and then to ascertain, after a sufficient time had been allowed for the experiment, whether any appreciable difference in the proportion of deaths to cures, and, if so, what, would be manifested as the result of united petitions to Heaven.

With this scheme I do not propose to deal yet a little. It may be propounded in the spirit of Voltaire, or in that of St. Francis when he offered himself to the ordeal of fire against the Egyptian Imâms; and therefore, although I shall presently discuss its evidential value, I confine myself, for the time, to investigating the intentions and arguments of its sponsor.

The paper coincides, in date of publication, with one by Prof. Beesly in "The Fortnightly Review," from which I extract the following passage, whose delicate humor and refined good feeling need no comment of mine: —

> "When Archbishop Tait claims to have effected the cure of the Prince of Wales by his Form of Public Prayer, issued to all churches and chapels in England and Wales, and in the town of Berwick-upon-Tweed, he is, in the eyes of most educated men, as much an impostor as Father Peter Conway driving a voter to the poll at the point of the sacrament, or a gypsy examining the hand of a kitchen-maid; and, to borrow a phrase from 'The Pall Mall Gazette,' 'not one whit less an impostor, because he believes in every word he says, in good faith.' All these avail themselves of their mysterious claims to extract money from the community; and, if the amount so extracted were to be the measure of criminality and of punishment, it is to be feared that Lambeth would come off worst."

I may digress for a moment, to point out that the logic of this expression of opinion is at fault from the lack of one essential quality, — that of true resemblance between the things compared.

On the one hand, there is neither evidence nor probability

that Archbishop Tait issued his form — which is simply neither better nor worse than the average of those very curious Lambeth prayers — as an infallible specific and spell. He did not say, even by implication, "Use this formula, and you will succeed; use any other, and you will probably fail." Nor, on the other hand, would his position and income have been affected in the smallest degree by popular neglect or acceptance of the document.

Prof. Tyndall has not been, on this occasion, as explicit as Mr. Beesly; but, some years ago (1865 and 1867), he uttered opinions in the very same periodical and in "The Pall Mall Gazette," which are identical in effect, however more courteously worded; and he has not subsequently retracted them. In one particular, he has gone even beyond his brother sceptic; for, while Prof. Beesly modestly contents himself with ranking on his side the "majority of educated persons" as disbelievers in the efficacy of prayer, Prof. Tyndall claimed the support of the "great majority of sane persons," and thus leaves the creed of a special providence not even the sympathies of a respectable minority of ignorant, albeit not unthinking, men; but will have it, that in the wise and charitable language of an anonymous though easily recognizable writer in "Fraser's Magazine," in 1866, "intelligent men have withdrawn from active participation in the whole matter; and enthusiasts, dreamers, knaves, and fools have now the field to themselves."

In order to appreciate Mr. Tyndall's objections at their

true value, it is only just to him and to myself to let him speak in his own words: —

"I turn to the account of the Epping cholera case, and learn that the people drank poisoned water. To alter by prayer the consequences of this or any similar fact, to deprive by petition even a single molecule of miasmatic matter of its properties, would, in the eye of science, be as much a miracle as to make the sun and moon stand still. For one of these results, neither of us would pray: on the same grounds, I refuse to pray for either." — *Pall Mall Gazette*, Oct. 19, 1865.

"They ask for fair weather and for rain, but they do not ask that water may run up hill; while the man of science clearly sees that the granting of one petition would be just as much an infringement of the law of conservation as the granting of the other. Holding the law to be permanent, he prays for neither."

I have an objection to allege on the threshold, before I proceed to show where I believe a fallacy to underlie these statements. It is, that Prof. Tyndall does not plainly say what theological ground he takes up. There are five different grounds, however, which may be taken up by disbelievers in prayer: —

1. They may be Atheists; in which case, prayer logically falls through for lack of an object, albeit it is maintained none the less by Comte in the very curious religion he invented.

2. They may be Pantheists; in which case, the things usually prayed against are to them as much parts of the

universally-diffused Divinity as their opposites, and, being necessary, are, of course, irremovable and irreformable.

3. They may be Theists, of that particular stamp which regards God in the light of a skilful mechanician, who after constructing the universe, and setting it at work, withdrew himself, thenceforward, from all interference with it, as completely as a clockmaker does in the instance of a clock which he has exported to a foreign country. Prayer here is useless, because God, under this theory, is not a party actively concerned, and will not interfere.

4. They may think themselves Christians, and then argue, either from the Calvinist point of view, that God has ordained all events whatsoever by an absolute and irreversible fiat, which can in no wise be affected by any entreaties of man;

5. Or else, what comes practically to the same thing, though not open to quite the same moral objections, they may urge that God, being supremely wise, just, loving, and merciful, ordains every thing in the very best way; so that, were he to alter his arrangements to meet man's ignorant wishes, he would have to alter them for the worse; and it is therefore the truest faith to leave the matter in his hands. This is the argument which Canon Kingsley adduced; not without a certain force, when the registrar-general's returns in 1861 showed that the cold, wet summer of 1860, which drew forth so many petitions for fair weather, had been exceptionally healthy for men and cattle; so that the average of deaths throughout England sank considerably.

These five grounds, though various enough to distinguish contrariant schools, are reducible to two, — Atheism and Necessism.

It is possible to take up yet another, the only one which is genuinely *sceptical*, in the true sense of that misused word, — that of the Agnostics, who frankly confess that they know nothing, and have very little expectation of ever knowing any thing, of the merits of the question on the one side or the other. But Prof. Tyndall's active crusade against prayer (albeit not easily reconcilable with another expression of his opinions, which I will cite presently) disallows him this position, and compels him to accept one of the other two.

If he is consciously arguing from the Atheistic side, I submit that he is bound to tell us so much. And, as the discussion is idle between persons who are not agreed on the existence of a God, I shall prefer to assume that Prof. Tyndall's objection comes from the Necessarian side.

And to Necessism there are some fatal objections. Whether it be taken to express the absolute unchangeability of God himself, or that of a system of laws devised by him, it is clear, that, if we once postulate it, we must allow the universality of its range and operation. We cannot argue that there must be fixity in one sphere, and yet that there may be contingency in another. Every thing must be part of the sequence of inevitable law; and nothing can be, or could have been, other than it is.

Now, I would just point out the circumstance, that, whether

this theory be true or false, every human being acts, and cannot help acting, on the hypothesis of its falsehood. The most fanatical disciple of Islam, the most philosophic Spinozist, although striving to accommodate himself to the practical recognition of destiny, cannot do it. He will eat when he is hungry, if food be attainable; he will go out of his way to cross a bridge, rather than attempt an untried ford right in the path; he will lock up his valuables if he anticipates theft. It is of no use to reply that his taking all these precautions against danger of any kind is as much pre-ordained as any thing else, for the fact remains that he is conscious of free choice in the matter; and no argument within himself, however ingenious its special pleading, will really convince him that he had no alternative, since, if there be a constraining force, it is absolutely imperceptible. Not only so; but there is an element of direct disproof, which is, that, wherever the fatalist theory avowedly prevails, we always find a very exceptional ratio of physical and mental apathy, as in Turkey and China, whence we are fairly entitled to argue that it is the known presence of this dogma which benumbs activity, since, were its operation really universal, mere ignorance of its existence would make no visible difference. Necessism, therefore, as a theory of life, being always and everywhere unworkable, is condemned as unthinkable too.

If we base the argument on God's immutability, we are the sport of an ambiguous expression. Moral fixity and perfection is necessary to our idea of God, but not so iron uniformity of action.

In truth, a moment's thought will show that to predicate absolute unchangeableness in all respects of him is to detract from his perfection, not to enhance it, since variety is a necessary integer in man's conception of absolute beauty. Change from what is in itself perfect need not be changed to less or more loveliness, as any one can tell who has watched the sunrises and sunsets of the Adriatic and the Archipelago, with their marvellous shifting and play of colors, alike in beauty, but diverse in chromatic expression. And, granted his existence as Creator and Lawgiver, sufficient evidence exists that he has been the Author of change. I interrogate the records of geology; and I find certain strata wherein no token of former life, no trace of organic remains, is discoverable. Moreover, science tells me, that, at the era indicated as that when these strata were formed, life was not only absent, but impossible. After a time, a change of the most momentous character is discernible. Life made its appearance on our globe, at first in vegetable forms, and later on in animal ones also. No ingenuity on the part of the extremer champions of evolution has yet shown that life can be evolved out of death. I will grant that some little progress has been made towards showing that organisms may possibly be developed out of inorganic bodies by a re-arrangement of molecules; but not one decillionth of an inch has yet been spanned of the unmeasured gulf which parts death and life, as modes of existence, from each other. Second only, if even second, to this inexplicable prodigy, is the sudden appearance of man upon the surface of the globe, differing, as he does, in essentials, more widely from the anthropoid apes than they do from the amœba and the rhizopod. Life and reason were once not on the earth. They are so now. What prodigy can be greater, what change more astonishing? If we could imagine a race of reasoning beings inspecting our globe from a neighboring planet, with instruments powerful enough to afford them a clear view of its surface, and carrying on their recorded observations for some centuries before the first vegetable sprang up, or the first saurian crawled, might we not also assume that they babbled inductive nonsense about "the necessary character of natural laws," and the impossibility of any change ever taking place?

For here comes in the deadliest argument of all against Necessism. It is an unreasoning and unreasonable hypothesis, and no more. I find myself, as a thinker, in frequent collision with the fact that men — educated and sane men, yes, and eminent physicists, too — will say the same thing in different words, and think, or try to make me think, that they have explained or accounted for it. We laugh at the story of the quack, who satisfied an old woman, who had long inquired in vain why her child was born dumb, by telling her that the reason was, that it had come into the world without the faculty of speech. But when a physicist tells me that the reason why oil and water will not mix, or why sulphuric-acid does not melt gold, is, that these substances have severally no chemical affinity for each other, he is doing exactly the same thing, and expecting me to be grateful for this increase to my stock of ideas. And this is the juggle which is played with the expression, "natural law." There is absolutely no intellectual process at work in the assertion that things will go on in the way that they have hitherto done; for I deny that any law making continuance necessary, or even probable, has been discovered, or that physicists have as yet established more than the fact that certain phenomena or acts come after one another in, as yet, invariable sequence. That the antecedent event is the cause, and the subsequent one the effect, no one has shown, far less *why* the results are such and such in any case. It is not reason, but mere brute instinct, which makes me expect sunrise to-morrow. Stars have, ere now, disappeared from the gaze of astronomers; and no man knows what has become of them, — whether they have been burnt out by some tremendous combustion, or carried away into space, or absorbed by attraction into some other orb; but they are gone. What intellectual reason can be given why the sun should not be the next to vanish? And, supposing he did, what would be the effect on our solar system? Of course, the answer given will be, "It is *certain* that the sun will rise to-morrow."

I am not disputing the fact, though I deny that the past

can prove the future; but the point I wish to urge is this: I am told by Prof. Tyndall and his friends, that the great majority of educated and sane men are at one as to the absolute invariability of natural law, and, by implication, that I am a dunce and a fool for believing that God can and does work miracles.

I will not trouble myself to disclaim the epithets; but I may fairly ask my scientific critics to deal with me as a teacher at Earlswood Asylum would do with any idiot whom he wished to instruct. The use of the terms "educated" and "sane" surely implies that the objection to a belief in the "miracles of prayer" is an intellectual one. If so, let us have it, by all means. But to say, "Such a thing has been hitherto, therefore it will continue to be," is not an intellectual proposition at all; and the word "therefore" has no business in it, for there is no minor term to the syllogism.

On the other hand, the argument for prayer is an intellectual one, and is based on a regular process of reasoning. The reasoning may be good or bad, conclusive or inconclusive; but, as a mere mental process, it stands on an immeasurably higher level than the bare unprovable assertion of Prof. Tyndall and the Necessarians, which has no loftier mental rank than the instinct which prompts some insects to lay up a winter-store of provisions.

I dwell upon this point, not out of soreness, nor from any desire for recrimination, but simply to press on public attention the defects of hazy thought and unbalanced expression, which mark this whole school in every thing unconnected with the idols of its cave. Take the very plea which is meant to impose on the jury before which the case is being tried. Is it not plain that the broad and unqualified allegation as to the opinions of the "great majority of sane and educated persons" can only be accounted for in one way,—that of using the words "educated and sane" in a novel and arbitrary sense, as equivalent to "holding the opinions of Profs. Tyndall and Beesly"? If the physicists had been men of a truly and universally scientific temper, they would have made an induction from the opinions of the "great majority of sane and educated men," I suppose, in Europe, America, and the various Colonies, leaving Africa and Asia out of consideration.

It would not, in the present condition of our race, have been necessary to examine much more than ten millions of people of all countries subject to the inquiry; and the Blue Book thus produced would be a highly interesting volume, but perhaps a little defective on the score of portability. No human being supposes that they have done this, or taken any steps towards doing it; and yet, till they have achieved something of the kind, they have no right to use loose talk of this sort about the numerical strength of their supporters.

When Canning asked the famous question, "Did you ever know a senior wrangler that wasn't a fool?" we may be sure he had no idea of casting a doubt on the success of the tripos as a test of mathematical faculty and acquirement.

What he possibly had in his mind, albeit he had, perhaps, not thought it out fully, is, that men who have devoted themselves exclusively to geometry and its branches, wherein necessary sequence does exist, and where contingency is totally absent, are singularly deficient in practical judgment. because they have never learnt to make allowance for unexpected events disturbing their calculation of futurity.

In like manner, the physicists seem unable to rise out of the plane of material conceptions into broad moral and spiritual views, or even to look at phenomena belonging to other spheres of knowledge with scientific eyes. They are like Jedidiah Buxton, the calculating boy of the last century, taken to see Garrick act Shakspeare, and coming away unimpressed alike by poet and actor, but being able to state with precision how many separate words Garrick uttered in the course of the drama.

One result of these very narrow sympathies is, that they live in a clique; and the cliquish temper makes them, as I have said, profoundly unscientific. To me possibly, as neither sane nor educated, every fact is a fact; and I do not see my way to ignoring any fact that comes in my way, and interferes with me in any fashion. As soon as Mr. Darwin's theory of "natural selection" is proved, I am ready to embrace it; and I am not in the least frightened at the word "evolution."

But Christianity seems to me quite as large and important a fact in the world as the existence of a cross-breed of pigeons, or the dropping-off of a tadpole's tail; and the belief in the efficacy of prayer is not only an inseparable integer of that form of belief, but of every other that rises above the lowest grade of savage Feticism. Now, here is an example of what I said about the difficulty physicists experience in facing any save material ideas. If you draw their attention to any very widely-spread and enduring practice affecting men's bodies, notably such matters as the use of fermented stimulants, or of narcotics, such as tobacco, opium, bhang, or betel, they will argue, and, as I think, quite justly, against teetotalers, that the very universality of the practice is an adequate proof that it fulfils some useful purpose in animal economy, and that, consequently, whatever may be said in favor of regulation, abolition would be an error.

But, transfer precisely the same argument to the plane of spiritual ideas, and they are at once incapable of applying the analogy. They allege that the presence of a whole world of aspirations and notions concerning a supernatural ideal, and the incontrovertible fact that men's morals and conduct are powerfully influenced by the shape which these aspirations and notions take, is no proof whatever that they are more than brain-phantasms, as unreal in their working as in their origin. This seems to me purely unphilosophical; for I can see no reason why prayer, as an actual fact in the universe, should not be investigated as patiently and exhaustively as tobacco.

And, while I am dealing with this point, I may draw attention to the noteworthy circumstance, that in proportion as we ascend in the scale of humanity, as we take a higher race in a higher stage of intellectual development, these notions and aspirations become more definite, more elaborate, more completely recognizant of orderly supernaturalism. We find Brahminism and Buddhism above the Fetish creeds; we see Mohammedanism rising in many particulars above them, and Christianity at the summit of the scale; that is, that, according as whole nations become more "sane and educated," the nearer they are to accepting the system which Mr. Tyndall urges us to reject; while it is only amongst the lowest savages, of races so degraded that the English idiot is incomparably more decent and teachable, that we find that absence of the belief and practice of prayer to God which is offered now as the ultimate test of superior wisdom. With all deference, I prefer the Aryan to the Andaman or the Papuan type; and I cannot see how a recurrence to the religious level of the latter can be other than fatuously retrograde.

I complain that the opponents of Christian prayer refuse to face these broad facts, and persist in ignoring them, as if that made them loom less large on the canvas of the world. They are bound, if they wish us to set aside truths of such visible magnitude and of such philosophical significance, to give us some sufficient reason for neglecting the successive strata of human thought, and the vigorous surface of living mental growth, and for concentrating our attention on the inorganic granite of Nihilism.

Again: I have said that I am not frightened at the word "evolution." But the word "supernatural" seems to startle an ordinary physicist into hysterics; and he has no presence of mind left after he has once heard it, or suspects its coming utterance. If he does listen to the sound for a moment, it is merely to assure us that it is exploded nonsense, and will vanish in a few years through the progress of science. Here, again, I must draw attention to a curiously unscientific attitude which physicists adopt towards psychology. They never can take in the simple fact that human nature, in its mental as well as its physical constitution, has been much the same as far back as our records testify. Hence they confuse two radically distinct notions,—that of the accumulation of human knowledge, and that of the advance of the human intellect. Nothing is commoner than to find a certain school of biblical critics starting as new and insurmountable some objection to the authenticity of some scriptural document which must, almost of necessity, have presented itself to the shrewd dialecticians who tasked the powers of the early Apologists, but which is imagined to be inaccessible to any save a modern intellect, as though that were something different in kind from an ancient one. And, conversely, we are told in very clear and unfaltering accents, that there are follies of belief and temperament, which have died out of inanition, as a result of mental growth through the ages; and that Christianity is one of these, and is going its way. They are perpetually crying out to us, —

> "Thou, too, shalt pass, Galilean: thy dead shall go down to their dead."

The cleverest exposition of this theory was in Mr. Lecky's "History of Rationalism in Europe," wherein the decadence, and, as it was alleged, the disappearance, of the belief in witchcraft, was treated at length as a palmary example. And now the Spiritualism of America, which does not differ one jot, in character or method, from the "white magic" of the middle ages, has spread with such force and rapidity, almost since Mr. Lecky's book appeared, as to count, amongst one of the most educated and hard-headed populations in the world, disciples variously estimated at from six to ten millions. I see no proofs of superiority in other matters. I had very much rather trust the statements, the inferences, the judgment, of Thucydides in any matter of history, than Mr. Froude's. I am sure Mr. Tyndall would not claim equality for his own powers with those of Aristotle, Bacon, or Newton (though the two latter were misguided enough to believe in supernaturalism, and were ignorant of many things which Mr. Tyndall knows); and I doubt whether any modern feats of engineering, as mere exemplifications of human skill and power, exceed the achievements of those who built the Pyramids, and raised the vast temples of Karnak and Luxor.

"The age culls simples,
With a broad clown's back turned broadly to the glory of the stars:
We are gods by our own reckoning, and may well shut up the temples,
And wield on, amid the incense-steam, the thunder of our cars.

And we throw out acclamations of self-thanking, self-admiring,
With, at every mile run faster, 'Oh the wondrous, wondrous age!'
Little thinking if we work our souls as nobly as our iron,
Or if angels will commend us at the goal of pilgrimage.

Why, what *is* this patient entrance into Nature's deep resources,
But the child's most gradual learning to walk upright without bane?
When we drive forth, from the cloud of steam, majestical white horses,
Are we greater than the first men who led black ones by the mane?

If we trod the depths of ocean, if we struck the stars in rising,
If we wrapped the globe intensely with one hot electric breath,
'Twere but power within our tether, no new spirit-power comprising;
And in life we were not greater men, nor bolder men in death."

Considerations such as these dispose, as it seems to me, of both the assertions, that belief in the supernatural is doomed, and that the coming doom is the result of the intellectual progress of mankind. And, moreover, if they did not, still these assertions belong to the sphere of unfulfilled prophecy; and it is with the present we have to deal, not with the future. The question is not, How will our posterity, in a millennary or so, account for the disappearance of Christianity? but, How is the present and continued existence of that belief to be intelligently accounted for now?

I think it must be allowed as a philosophical axiom, that the fact of any thing continuing to live is a proof that it has vitality in it, and that such vitality must be as true as any other fact in the physical or moral universe, and, therefore, as fitting matter for scientific inquiry. Now, if the word "supernatural" be looked at dispassionately, its terrors disappear. They exist only in the imagination of those who persist in limiting the word "natural" to such matters as fall within the sphere of sensible observation, and who, if they recall the speech once made by a young man to Dr. Parr, "I make a rule never to believe any thing I do not understand," also remind one of the answer, "Then your creed will be one of the shortest on record." What we mean by supernatural is no more than that the thing spoken of belongs to a higher plane in creation than its surroundings. In a world of granite, a solitary plant would be supernatural; for it would possess the unshared attributes of life and growth. In a purely mineral and vegetable world, an animal endowed with motion and volition would be supernatural; and man was supernatural when he appeared first in the world which lacked him as its head. No preceding causes could account for these several manifestations; but, when once admitted and tabulated, they fell within the recognized order of Nature. All, therefore, that is implied in the word "supernatural" is the belief (not necessarily absurd in itself), that there may be existences higher in the scale of being than man, and capable, in perfectly orderly fashion, of achievements which as far surpass his as the construction of the most intricate machinery (for instance, that used in making cards for wool, or in Mr. Babbage's famous engine) exceeds the skill of the beaver. A miracle does not mean a reversal of existing laws, but the manifestation of some law unknown to and inexplicable by man, and can be declared impossible only on the hypothesis that there is no God, or that God is not a free agent.

Take Mr. Tyndall's two examples, as cited earlier in this paper,— the folly of praying that miasma may be neutralized, or that water may run up hill. These would be impossible miracles to an ape. I can perform them any day I please. I pour a few drops of a wholesome disinfectant into the poisoned water, and I can drink it with safety. I rig a force-pump, and drive the reluctant fluid up through pipes to the top of the loftiest mansion, and, lo! there are the two miracles worked. If God gave chemists the wisdom to invent disinfectants, if he disclosed the secret of the pump to Torricelli, why cannot he do the like himself, at times, without revealing his processes? Must he, of necessity, work through human agency? or does it follow, that, where human agency is visible, there can have been no antecedent prayer?

Neither of these questions can be answered, save by the high *à priori* method, which is not very convincing to logicians. And to take no notice of them is, in fact, to fall back on the unavowed principle of Atheism; for the distinction between the natural and supernatural does not belong to Scripture, to theology, nor to man's original consciousness. It is a mere artificial product of modern speculation, and need not have, most probably has not, any true existence in the world of being. To the Christian philosopher, the words indicate no more than the known and the unknown operations of the same Almighty God; and the estimate he forms of them is, that as all the known operations are orderly, and free from arbitrary caprice, so the unknown ones are presumably the like. And it is no more difficult or unreasonable to suppose the immediate cure of blindness or paralysis, given an adequate reason for it, than to acknowledge the ordinary fact of the development of a fully sentient human being out of an embryonic germ, since each equally surpasses our power, and baffles our investigation.

I have said that the doctrine of prayer, unlike the assertion of invariable sequence, is the result of intelligent thought; but I have not yet shown why it is so. The facts of geology establish, as I have said, that change is not, in itself, alien to the Divine Mind. Yet no help is gained, so far, towards meeting the objections of those who allow God's freedom from all restraint, save that of the necessity of his own perfections, but who argue, that, though he *can* change, he will not, because he already orders all things for the best. This is the subtlest form of Necessism, but is met at once by the problem of evil, moral and physical. Unless we fall back on that form of Pantheism which sees in evil as much a part of God as in good, we are forced to confess a permitted antagonism in the universe; and we find in any case, that a great part of our own intellectual and moral progress is reached through the conflict with evil, and through our efforts to banish or neutralize its malign influence. Unless our reflective faculties are in a very apathetic or a very degraded state, we recognize this conflict, apart from its salutary effect on ourselves, as a duty to God and to society; that is, we employ ourselves in doing what, on the Necessarian theory, is simply thwarting God's will, since, if he did not mean evil to continue, he would not fail to destroy it himself. And, consequently, no one acts on this theory in morals any more than in the practical concerns of life, — sowing and reaping, and such like provisions for physical needs; so that it, too, is universally rejected, and therefore ultimately unthinkable.

What does this establish? Simply that we constantly base our action on the fact that not every thing is in the best possible state, but that most things may be and ought to be bettered. If we do so, there is nothing inconsistent, but rather the reverse, in asking God to help us in so bettering what we think to be wrong or evil. And as the Christian Scriptures, in common with the Jewish, constantly inculcate the duty of prayer as an element of the war with evil, it seems hardly open to members of any Christian body to question its utility. Further: even the Necessarian view does not logically exclude prayer, though it seems to do so;

for it is perfectly conceivable that God may have ordained prayer as a necessary preliminary to the obtaining certain results, and that it enters into his system of pre-arrangement in a manner which may be compared, in some degree, to the use of stamped paper to give civil validity to certain documents amongst us. An unstamped receipt for sums of a certain value is inadmissible in our courts as evidence of payment, and even exposes the signatory to a heavy fine, albeit it is just as complete historical and moral evidence as the stamped receipt. The object with us is to increase national revenue with the least onerous incidence of taxation; and God's object in requiring prayer may very well be as simple and practical, though the direct motive on man's part may be merely the obtaining of desired benefits.

Now, this object on God's part must needs be a moral one, unless we are content to form a low estimate of his nature. It cannot be the mere desire to promote his own glory (which is, or used to be, the hyper-Calvinist explanation), since that would bring him down to the moral level of Nebuchadnezzar, or any similar Oriental despot who claims the adoration of his subjects. And, moreover, such an explanation would not cover the area of human prayer, since populous nations which have no knowledge of the God of the Bible are none the less in the habit of making petitions to unseen and superhuman powers. The vast and almost universal extent of this tendency cannot be philosophically accounted for in any fashion which does not recognize the necessary function of prayer in satisfying certain inherent desires of man. Those desires are to know, or at least feel after, something higher, stronger, nobler, than himself, to obtain its sympathy, and to shelter himself under its protection; in the spirit of Wellington's despatch immediately after Waterloo, "I have escaped unhurt: the finger of Providence was upon me." Now, Feticism which is in some of its forms very closely allied to the modern theology of physicists, in that it deifies the brute forces of Nature, stands lowest amongst religions, precisely because it does not reach to the notion of divine personality. Hydraulic and electric force are stronger and more enduring than I; but they can only incidentally affect me: whereas I can govern and direct them, through the conduit, along the telegraph-wires, down the lightning-conductor. I may use them, I may sometimes fear them; but I cannot apply such language as love, trust, or sympathy to my feelings towards them, or any other natural forces. They do not and can not satisfy my intellectual and moral cravings, which require a Person to content them, precisely because I am conscious that my own personality, which puts me so much higher in the scale of creation than any impersonal or unreasoning force, must come from a Person who is at least as high over me as I am over a galvanic current. Were it otherwise, man would be, in the fullest sense of the word, self-sufficient, and would find his ideal in the noblest of his own race; but that is not true, even under the Comtist worship of humanity. It has become necessary for it to treat the most famous of mankind merely as inferior saints of a calendar, and to invent a Frankenstein monster, a personification of aggregate mankind, as the supreme object of worship, in order to cheat that hunger of the soul after a perfect Man, which Christianity alone can assuage, because it alone tells us that this perfect Man is also perfect God, and thus brings into harmonious contact two ideas otherwise parted and irreconcilable.

If we take from man this craving for worship, and throw him back on himself alone for his ideal, all history tells us, that brute force and material prosperity become the only recognized good. Therefore it is part of God's moral education of man to keep the craving alive, to lead men onwards by setting before them the loftiest conceivable standard, to soften hardness and to abase pride by teaching man that the All-Holy is also the All-Merciful, that the Most High is also the most lowly, in that he rejects no suitor, and scorns no intercourse.

But there is only one way to prevent the craving from wearing itself out; and that is by satisfying it, at least occasionally. If it be conceded (as it must on any theistic hypothesis) that God has implanted the longing in us, then it follows, as a necessary consequence of his nature, that he will not cheat his petitioners. If the experience of mankind were, that he neither heard nor answered prayer, there is small probability that its prevalence would still be well-nigh universal.

On the contrary, the whole induction is immeasurably the other way, and asserts that God always does hear, and always does answer, devout and trustful prayer, albeit he may not always grant the special petition of any given worshipper. Here is another case in which unscientific prejudice has barred honest investigation. It is the plainest duty of any man who undertakes to demonstrate the inefficacy of prayer, to inquire into the results ascribed to devout intercession by all sincere Christians. It would be easy enough for a truly impartial investigator to apply for data to a certain number of ministers of religion, belonging to different societies, and to ask them to send in details of cases which satisfy the following conditions: —

1. Extreme need of obtaining some benefit seemingly or really inaccessible, by ordinary means, to the person in want.

2. Devout prayer on behalf of the said person, whether offered by himself or by others.

3. The obtaining the desired benefit in an unforeseen manner, subsequently to the prayer.

I do not at all mean to suggest that only cases of this sort are likely to represent answers to prayer, nor yet to assert categorically that 2 and 3 must needs be connected together as cause and effect; but what I urge is, that, if some hundreds or thousands of such cases are discoverable (a thing of which I have no doubt whatever), the number of the coincidences would raise a very strong presumption in favor of the Christian theory, and be evidence of exactly the same kind as is relied on by physicists; that is, that extremely frequent sequence of two events argues a connection between them, though it cannot exactly prove it. I assert, in common with all men who have had any wide spiritual experience, that such answers to prayer are amongst the ordinary facts of religion, and that it is the plainest duty of any one who denies their existence, to base his objection on inductive disproof, not on *à priori* theories which are simply contradicted by other *à priori* theories that satisfy a larger number of mental wants. For, as I have pointed out again and again, the Necessarian doctrine really means that God is not a free agent, and makes the highest manifestation of him to lie in unbroken uniformity: whereas, the other *à priori* conception of God as a moral governor of the universe assumes, as I think more reasonably, that he would take pains to make his creatures sure of his existence, — a thing he can effect in no way conceivable to us, save by convincing us, through some superhuman act of his which we cannot reduce under any known law, that the only necessity is his will, and that his laws are neither identical with himself, nor superior over him. Such an act, when made to draw attention to some spiritual teaching, and having, therefore, a definite aim, we call a miracle.

And, unless we are prepared to deny our own powers and operations, we cannot logically or reasonably refuse this power of working miracles to God. I have already shown how man's skill can deal with the two tasks which Prof.

Tyndall thinks are too great for God. But let us take achievements on a much larger scale. If it were recorded in the Bible, that two men, ten thousand miles apart, were enabled to communicate with each other instantaneously, and thus practically annihilate space, is there the smallest doubt that the whole ruck of unbelievers, in days before the electric telegraph, would have ridiculed the story as an Oriental hyperbole? Or let us take another kind of example. Readers of old English chroniclers are familiar with the accounts given of the soil, the climate, the flora, and the fauna of the East-Anglian counties, as they were in the middle ages. Embankment, draining, and cultivation have changed all four, and that in no petty degree, but radically. Man has brought another set of laws and conditions to bear upon a large tract of country, and has changed the very face of Nature thereby. And, conversely, man's neglect has made a pestilential desert of the Roman Campagna, once thickly set with gardens, farms, and dwellings. Yet we are told to believe that God cannot do what man does on so great a scale, or, what comes to the same thing, that he will not do what he instructs and empowers man to do. For here is the dilemma for Necessarians who plead God's changelessness. Either God wills an unalterable state of things, or he does not. If he does, then man is able to counteract him, and is so far stronger than he: if he does not, the argument, from invariable sequence, falls to the ground.

There is, however, a sub-form of the same objection which I have not yet directly met, although it is already answered by implication. I mean that drawn from God's omniscience. Granted that he can, and even may, change his apparent course of dealing with men, why should it be necessary for them to tell him their wants, seeing that he knows them already, and is just and loving enough to fulfil such as are commendable or reasonable?

The answer is, that prayer is not for God's instruction, but for ours. It is to teach us dependence on him, not to inform him of any thing whereof he may be presumed ignorant. And, besides, this objection is only the *à priori* fallacy again. If we base our belief in God's omniscience on Holy Writ, then that revelation declares as fully his requirement of prayer as it does any thing else concerning him: if we base it merely on our own conceptions of what suits the character of God, then we find ourselves faced by the necessity of also attributing direct sympathy with us to him; and sympathy without intercourse is a delusion.

There is yet another aspect of prayer which is too important to be omitted. I mean its reflex action on those who habitually practise it. So salutary is it seen to be even by unbelievers, that Comte has been forced to import it as an incongruous exotic into his system, lest his disciples should lack its influence; and even Prof. Tyndall has committed himself to approval of it in very emphatic language. He says, —

"While prayer is thus inoperative in external nature, it may re-act with beneficial power on the human mind. . . . And if our spiritual authorities could only devise a form in which the heart might express itself, without putting the intellect to shame, they might utilize a power which they now waste, and make prayer, instead of a butt to the scorner, the potent inner supplement of a noble life."

Merely premising that the use of the word "power" in this sentence shows that the word "prayer" cannot here be taken as equivalent to praise or worship, but must mean a force of some kind brought to bear on God, that is, petition or intercession, I ask, in unfeigned perplexity, What ever does Prof. Tyndall mean?

He has told us that he refuses to pray for any interference with natural laws; and moral questions are so bound up with physical ones, that I fail to see how he could consistently ask for any change of temperament for himself or others; so that altogether, bearing in mind the limitations he puts on divine power, I am at a loss to guess what kind of a God he is willing to pray to, or what kind of blessings he is prepared to pray for.

For myself, I can conceive no more immoral sham than going through a process of the sort, fully conscious that I did not expect any result from my petitions, except such as might arise from temporary excitement; and that I was degrading man's highest privilege, that of sacred communion with his Maker, to the level of a fit of voluntary hysterics over the fictitious sorrows of a sentimental novel.

If, as seems conceded, prayer actually does produce a beneficial effect on those who practise it, no explanation is valid or reasonable which does not admit the truth of its fundamental notion, — that there is a superhuman Being who hears and answers prayer; for a mere delusion cannot produce tangible and recurrent results. Imagination is a powerful agent, no doubt, and has often wrought singular effects on the nervous system; but I do not know of any evidence in proof of the permanence of such effects; for, unless I mistake, the fancied benefit mostly disappears with the temporary excitement. But, in this case, a habit is generated, a gradual transformation of mind is brought about, and the whole man is lifted into a higher and purer atmosphere; while the incendiary assassins of the Parisian Commune help us to guess what kind of morality is developed by the negation of prayer.

And now to say another word about Prof. Tyndall's crucial examples. Let us suppose that he had chosen them more happily, and that he had taken a prayer for the suspension of the law of gravity, or something analogous, as a type of petition which Christians do not employ. His corollary from such abstention is, that we are inconsistent and unscientific, because we refrain from asking certain things which we regard as impossible, while we ask for other things which in the eyes of science are equally impossible. This is merely another instance of his lack of clear thought. When God has revealed his will distinctly to us in the order of nature, our duty as affectionate children and loyal subjects imposes on us the obligation of conforming ourselves to that will. But where he has not so disclosed his intentions, and where contingency may enter in, we are surely reasonable, not foolish, in asking that he may help us in his own way.

For example, if we saw a child thrusting its hand into a red-hot fire, we should scarcely pray that the fire might lose its scorching power, since that would be asking God to reverse his own laws. But if we sent up a cry that a sudden downpour of rain, such as often occurs, might extinguish the flame in time, or, failing that, should entreat for a blessing on the medical remedies employed, where would be the unscientific attitude? For as yet science has not laid down meteorological or pathological laws with such accuracy as to declare that they move in unchangeable cycles, or to assure us, that, given certain antecedents, certain consequents must undoubtedly follow; and I see no more impossibility in God's way to prevent him from directing a thunderstorm over a burning mass than there is in mine to hinder me from using a fire-engine for the same purpose. I may add, as an exhaustive refutation of this charge of inconsistency against Christians, that, while they firmly believe that Christ raised certain persons from the dead, they yet do not ask for the resuscitation of deceased friends, because they also believe that his ordinary will is that they should die; and therefore they conform themselves humbly to that will, though, up to the actual moment of death, they may often prolong their entreaties for recovery.

We are, in short, reasonable beings, praying to a reasonable God, and believing in the correlation of moral forces; and that is the true reason for rejecting the scheme for a prayer-gauge propounded by Mr. Tyndall's anonymous correspondent. That gentleman has indeed pointed out one scientific objection to his own proposal, which would deprive it, even were quantitative analysis of prayer a possibility, of any value as a test. I mean the impracticability of isolating the wards, so that the influence of prayer should be concentrated on one only. But, setting aside this consideration, the moral defect of the scheme is that which is really fatal to it.

It degrades worship and prayer to the rank of a magical incantation, and God to a being weak enough to be inthralled and compelled by such an influence.

This notion prevails in the Brahmin system. It is there held, that certain rites and sacrifices have an inherent power in themselves to sway the gods, altogether apart from the moral character or religious intention of the offerer, and that it is even possible, given the knowledge and opportunity, for a man not merely to subject his deities to his own will, but to dethrone them, and assume their place and attributes. Readers of the "Curse of Kehama" will need no digression on this head. But the God of Christians is a Being at once omnipotent, omniscient, and perfectly moral. He cannot be constrained, he may not be deceived, he will not lend himself to such a juggle; yet, that the experiment should have even an initial value or interest, it would be necessary that he should have given his assent to its being tried, either by open sign or by express revelation. The plagues of Egypt, the contest between Elijah and the priests of Baal, are examples of what I mean. But nothing now empowers us to accept such a challenge, were it even morally defensible; for the precept which binds us in all such matters is, "Thou shalt not tempt the Lord thy God." A writer in "The Spectator" of July 6, 1872, has with much shrewdness pointed out another objection, which is, that answer is promised only to sincere, devout, single-minded prayer; but that such a scheme as this necessarily involves insincerity and double-mindedness, since the recovery of the patients, nominally asked, is not the real motive of the petitioners, who are merely trying to prove and show off their personal influence with God.

There is yet another reason against the plan: it is that we cannot quantify prayer any more than we can poetry, art-feeling, or any other lofty and imponderable gift. I mean that there is no such thing as equality in the value of intercession. It does not follow at all, that, if you have one person praying for a thing, and ten persons praying for another thing, the calculus of probability is ten times in favor of the second petition. If this were so, prayer would be a mere mechanical force, and of no ethical value or significance whatever.

There is such a thing as a gift of prayer, just as there is of dramatic or artistic faculty. I do not mean the power, common in almost every Nonconformist pulpit, of making rhetorical addresses of a more or less devotional kind to the Deity, but that "effectual fervent prayer of a righteous man," or woman, which, as an apostle tells us, "availeth much." I have known, within my own experience, a few persons with whom it was a common thing to ask in prayer for various matters, and to get them. I do not assert that the prayer brought the desired blessings; but I do allege that the coincidences, if purely accidental, were more wonderful and inexplicable than the hypothesis of a God who can hear and answer his worshippers. Now, on the quantitative theory, this fact would introduce such a disturbance into the calculation, that no trustworthy results could be obtained. One petition from some unknown saint on behalf of the neglected wards, might outweigh in spiritual efficacy the aggregate intercessions of the forces concentrated on the experiment.

Further: it happens that I employed myself, some considerable time ago, in speculating what would be the practical result on modern unbelief, of a public revival of miracles. I have put before me the hypothesis of my being myself invested with a supernatural power of healing, and have asked myself what would come of it, assuming that the number and notoriety of the cures forced the physicists to take the matter up, and inquire into it, instead of dismissing it with contemptuous incredulity. And I became satisfied, that unless the power were universal and persistent in me, that is, that no case failed, under any conditions, its evidential value would be superciliously disregarded. The objectors would insist on God's working so as to please them. They would require a variety of specified conditions to be fulfilled in every instance, bargaining for the nature and duration of the disease, the character and number of witnesses to be present, the uniform repetition of the cure under carefully diversified circumstances, and the like. Then, if God did not choose to submit himself to such critics, or withdrew after a time the power conferred, they would look to the cessation of the miracle, not to its previous persistence, and reject it accordingly, as a mere abnormal phenomenon, not deserving of serious attention; while, on the other hand, even if it did continue, they would, I am convinced, ascribe it to the discovery on my part of some hidden pathological law, and would deny the existence of any superhuman causation. The evangelists are careful to let us know that the miracles they ascribe to Christ were so far from converting his chief opponents, that they merely imbittered their hostility. And I consequently do not believe for a moment, that even if the proposed experiment were one which is lawful for a Christian to try, if it were carried out to the letter, as suggested, and if the tabulated result should exhibit an enormous percentage of cures in the favored ward, that the hyper-dogmatic asserters of the impossibility of miracles would be convinced. They would whisper about, that one of the physicians had got a secret specific somehow, and was in league with the parsons to palm off his success as theirs; and they would probably point their remarks by showing how very conceivably that trick might have been played when chloroform was discovered, but not yet currently known.

The temper of Naaman, going away in a rage when told to avail himself of a secondary remedy divinely indicated, while he expected the pomp and dramatic circumstance of a public miracle, is common still. Reading the letter of Prof. Tyndall's correspondent between the lines, it seems to me to come from the pen of a materialist surgeon or physician; more probably the former. Now, as a theologian, I hold and teach that God works, as a rule, mediately rather than immediately upon men; and I think I can show a much simpler and more scientific test of the effect of prayer on the healing of the sick than the one proposed.

I mean, and all skilled pathological experience will bear me out, that first-rate nursing is almost, if not quite, equal to first-rate medical advice in curative value. First-rate nursing cannot be had, save as a rare exception, from the class whence the Gamps and Prigs of our hospitals are, or used to be, recruited. It tasks all the refinement, tact, and educated sympathy of a lady to raise it to the highest level. Several years ago Sir Edward Parry strove hard to get nurses of this stamp to volunteer for Haslar Hospital. Not one was forthcoming. But the powerful religious movement which is revolutionizing the Church of England before our eyes has since created the desired class; and several hospitals, notably that of University College, London, are now nursed by Sisters of conventual societies, who are moved by piety to their labor of love, and sustained in it by prayer. Would not a tabular comparison of the results severally attained by nurses who work for God, and nurses who work for money, be of some value as a basis of calculation? I desire to enforce my argument, that, as prayer is unquestionably the motive-power which produces the Sister of Mercy, it must be credited with the benefit a patient derives from having her at his bedside. Nor is this plea weakened by any allegation that a very much improved class of nurses, working primarily and avowedly for payment, can now be had; because the rehabilitation of nursing as a profession, the lifting it up out of the grade of drunken beldames to be the fit occupation of refined ladies, was the work of praying men and women, and of them only, whether we trace the English movement back to St. Vincent de Paul, Pastor Fliedner, or Miss Sellon.

I do not charge the physicists with any exceptional perverseness in their attitude towards religious questions. I simply note the facts, that any exclusive devotion to one particular range of study has a necessarily narrowing influence upon the intellect; and that physical science, like law, requires for its mastery such undivided and unremitting attention, that it is well-nigh impossible for its fervent devotees to be men of wide culture, and broad, statesman-like intelligence. The superior mechanical accuracy of execution obtained in the industrial arts by the minute division of labor in modern times has its compensating drawbacks in the extreme difficulty which is experienced in obtaining the harmony of idea and effect of earlier work, where the whole design, and the chief toil of elaboration, proceeded from a single brain and hand. Similarly, when the range of human knowledge was so far limited, that it was not a wild impossibility for a great and laborious intellect to survey it all, the leaders of scientific thought, the Aquinases, the Bacons, the Descartes, were able to see all forms of knowledge as parts of an harmonious whole. But now, when a man devotes forty years of patient study to butterflies or to *confervæ*, he does much to enlarge the store of facts at our disposal; but he inevitably cramps his own intellect in the process, and becomes incapable of giving a valuable opinion on any subject outside his routine. And the special stumbling-block in the way of physicists is, that the very fascination of their favorite pursuit blinds them altogether to its subordinate position in the domain of knowledge; for as the study of organic bodies ranks higher in complexity and interest than that of inorganic ones, as botany stands above mineralogy, and zoölogy over botany, so the loftiest range of all earthly science must needs be the investigation of the highest conceptions of the highest of animals, man.

Failing to understand this, they act as intelligently as a mineralogist would do, if he totally refused to allow the problem of life, because his own subjects of study are inorganic. Human physiology leads up, by inevitable process, to human psychology; and, when we reach that point, we are faced by the existence of prayer, not in the lowest, but in the highest natures.

A really scientific temper would say, "The fact of the existence of this phenomenon entitles it to respectful consideration. The fact that all inquiry in lower spheres of knowledge testifies to the truth of normal sequence, perhaps of law, makes it antecedently probable that prayer also belongs to a sphere of law, and has a definite purpose in the economy of the universe; since, if it had no such purpose, it would not, and could not, exist at all. Therefore, instead of irrationally denying its efficacy, let us examine its practical operation, without insisting on deductively accommodating it to a preconceived hypothesis."

Now, the preconceived hypothesis which underlies the whole argument against prayer is, that God, if there be a God, is only a collective name for an aggregate of blind, irrational, and inevitable forces, not a rational and moral Being, endowed with perfect free-will as an agent. Mr. J. S. Mill's clear brain sees this truth; and, in marked contradistinction to the narrow dogmatism of Prof. Tyndall, he allows at once that the existence of a personal God is fatal to any objection against miracles. He says in his "System of Logic, "In the case of an alleged miracle, the assertion is, that the effect was defeated, not in the absence, but in consequence, of a counteracting cause; namely, a direct interposition of an act of the will of some Being who has power over nature, and, in particular, of a Being whose will, being assumed to have endowed all the causes with the powers by which they produce their effects, may well be supposed able to counteract them. A miracle (as was justly observed by Brown) is no contradiction to the law of cause and effect: it is a new effect supposed to be introduced by the introduction of a new cause. Of the adequacy of that cause, if present, there can be no doubt; and the only antecedent improbability which can be ascribed to the miracle is the improbability that any such cause existed."

I may cite, in considering the supposed improbability, those true words of a poet I have already quoted: —

> "And this age shows, to my thinking, still more infidels to Adam,
> Than directly, by profession, simple infidels to God."

For the true philosophical deduction from the posited view, that man, despite his rational faculties, his free-will, and his high aspirations, is but the sport and plaything of blind, irrational forces, against which he is powerless to contend, and which have no moral power to pity or help him, is that, in like manner, the thinking part of man must needs be subjected to the instincts and passions of his animal nature; so that the gratification of his appetites becomes the loftiest goal of his ambition. It is not only the philosophical deduction, but the practical issue, as La Mettrie, Lagrange, and to some extent Diderot, established alike by precept and example.

The loftier spiritual philosophy argues, with Kant, that the supreme good consists of two factors, — supreme virtue and supreme happiness; and that, to realize the latter, we must admit the immortality of the soul, and, for the former, the existence of God. And, to establish that harmony of relation between the physical and moral world which is necessary to fully developed happiness, we are compelled to assert that this God is the common source and cause of both nature and morality.

Now, let us push the inquiry a step further, in the spirit of another great thinker, Hegel. What is good, not in the abstract, but concretely, to me? It is the union of the particular subjective will with the universal objective will; it is the volition of true reason in its purest form; it is Christ saying for himself, and teaching us to say, "Father, thy will be done." It follows, therefore, that we cannot construct, even in thought, a moral world without the introduction of prayer, which is the conscious reference of our needs and perplexities to a higher power and a purer reason than our own, and that if a true harmony of the universe exists at all, if it be no anarchic chaos, but a cosmic order, — the conclusion to which all theories of law point, — there must not only be a correlation of physical forces and a correlation of moral forces, but the physical and moral forces must be also mutually correlated, so that prayer legitimately enters as a kindred ally, not as a foreign and unlicensed intruder, into the domain of natural law.

I cannot forbear from citing some trenchant paragraphs from Emerson, which seem to me to drive this argument home: —

"The cure for false theology is mother-wit. Forget your books and traditions, and obey your moral perceptions at this hour. That which is signified by the words 'moral' and 'spiritual' is a lasting essence, and, with whatever illusions we have loaded them, will certainly bring back the words, age after age, to their ancient meaning. I know no words that mean so much. In our definitions, we grope after the *spiritual* by describing it as invisible. The true meaning of *spiritual* is *real,* — that law which executes itself, which works without means, and which cannot be conceived as not existing. Men talk of 'mere morality,' which is much as if one should say, 'Poor God, with nobody to help him!' I find the omnipotence and omnipresence in the re-action of every atom in nature. . . . Our recent culture has been in natural science. We have learned the manners of the sun and of the moon, of the rivers, the rains, of the mineral and elemental kingdoms, of plants and animals. Man has learned to weigh the sun, and its weight neither loses nor gains. The path of a star, the moment of an eclipse, can be determined to the fraction of a second. Well, to him the book of history, the book of love, the lures of passion, and the commandments of duty are opened; and the next lesson taught is the continuation of the inflexible law of matter into the subtle kingdom of will and of thought; that if, in sidereal ages, gravity and projection keep their craft, and the ball never loses its way in its wild path through space, a secreter gravitation, a secreter projection, rule not less tyrannically in human history, and keep the balance of power from age to age unbroken. For though the new element of freedom and an individual has been admitted, yet the primordial atoms are prefigured, and predetermined to moral issues, are in search of justice, and ultimate right is done. Religion, or worship, is the attitude of those who see this unity, intimacy, and sincerity; who see, that, against all appearances, the nature of things works for truth and right forever." [1]

It seems to me that ministers of religion are more to blame than any other class for the doubts which have been cast on the efficacy of prayer. Prof. Tyndall's correspondent, after a few words on the prevalence of prayer for the sick, adds, that, "in the larger and more ancient section of the church, prayer still continues on behalf of the deceased,—a custom, perhaps, not less pious and reasonable than the first-named."

To refuse these prayers, as is done by large numbers of persons who do not accept the entire Christian code, is to exhibit unbelief as deep and real as Prof. Tyndall's, though not covering so large an area. For it amounts to this, that they deny God's power in the realm of spirit as truly as Prof. Tyndall denies it in the realm of matter, since they virtually teach that the disembodiment of the soul terminates God's ability to influence it, and that it thus passes, for all practical purposes, out of his jurisdiction. This is the ne-

[1] Emerson's Essays on the Conduct of Life: Worship.

gation of omnipotence, the negation of progress, and, ultimately, the negation of immortality, and ought, if men were logical, which they happily are not, to lead to the rejection of Christianity altogether.

There is another particular in which the laxity and bad faith of the ministers of religion work to the same end. I mean the habitual omission of intercessory prayer, save at the distant intervals of Sunday worship. The English Church, in common with the other ancient communions of Christendom, enjoins upon all her clergy, whether parochial or not, the daily recitation of certain offices, which are largely intercessory, and further enjoins those who have parochial charges to give facilities to their congregations for daily assembling to the same end.

But the great majority, on no avowed plea whatever save personal sloth, evade, refuse, or even deride, the performance of this plain obligation; and it is only the other day that the Ritual Commission, in the interests of those who have systematically violated their voluntary pledges during the whole of their clerical career, endeavored to nullify this provision by a diluting rubric, which involved a moral bull of a very remarkable kind, to the effect that the object of the provision in question was merely to testify to the value set by the Church of England on daily prayer and intercession, and therefore that indolent clergymen might, for the future, testify the value they set upon it by omitting it at their pleasure.

The only deduction possible from such an attitude is, that

all persons who adopt it really consider prayer as a decent but nugatory form, to be employed as rarely as can well be contrived without coming into abrupt collision with vulgar prejudice; since, if they really did believe in its prevalence with God, and had any clear prospect of the mass of moral and physical evil with which they are surrounded, they would say, in the words of Isaiah, "I have set watchmen upon thy walls, O Jerusalem, which shall never hold their peace day nor night: ye that are the Lord's remembrancers, keep not silence, and give him no rest till he make Jerusalem a praise in the earth." This would be true belief and true brotherhood, and would carry into action those noble words of a living bard: —

"But thou,
If thou shouldst never see my face again,
Pray for my soul. More things are wrought by prayer
Than this world dreams of. Wherefore let thy voice
Rise like a fountain for me, night and day.
For what are men better than sheep or goats
That nourish a blind life within the brain,
If, knowing God, they lift not hands of prayer
Both for themselves and those who call them friend?
For so the whole round earth is every way
Bound by gold chains about the feet of God."

RICHARD FREDERICK LITTLEDALE.

IV.

STATISTICAL INQUIRIES INTO THE EFFICACY OF PRAYER.

By FRANCIS GALTON, F. R. S.

In the same month of August, 1872, in which Dr. Littledale replied to Mr. Tyndall in "The Contemporary," Mr. Galton brought re-enforcements to the attacking party by this article in "The Fortnightly Review," John Morley, editor, Chapman & Hall, publishers, 193 Piccadilly, vol. xii., new series, xviii., old series, No. lxviii., pp. 125–135.

Mr. Galton gained a certain position by his book on "Hereditary Genius: an Inquiry into its Laws and Consequences," published in 1869. His recent volume on "English Men of Science, their Nature and Nurture," is written to support Darwinism in its application to the human species. Mr. Galton gives us pedigrees in this last volume, from which it appears that he is own cousin to Mr. Darwin.

IV.

STATISTICAL INQUIRIES INTO THE EFFICACY OF PRAYER.

AN eminent authority has recently published a challenge to test the efficacy of prayer by actual experiment. I have been induced, through reading this, to prepare the following memoir for publication, nearly the whole of which I wrote and laid by many years ago, after completing a large collection of data, which I had undertaken for the satisfaction of my own conscience.

The efficacy of prayer seems to me a simple, as it is a perfectly appropriate and legitimate, subject of scientific inquiry. Whether prayer is efficacious or not, in any given sense, is a matter of fact on which each man must form an opinion for himself. His decision will be based upon data more or less justly handled, according to his education and habits. An unscientific reasoner will be guided by a confused recollection of crude experience. A scientific reasoner will scrutinize each separate experience before he admits it as evidence, and will compare all the cases he has selected on a methodical system.

The doctrine commonly preached by the clergy is well expressed in the most recent, and by far the most temperate and learned, of theological encyclopædias; namely, "Smith's Dictionary of the Bible." The article on "Prayer," written by the Rev. Dr. Barry, states as follows: "Its real objective efficacy . . . is both implied and expressed (in Scripture) in the plainest terms. . . . We are encouraged to ask special blessings, both spiritual and temporal, in hopes that thus, and thus only, we may obtain them. . . . It would seem the intention of Holy Scripture to encourage all prayer, more especially intercession, in all relations and for all righteous objects." Dr. Hook, the present Dean of Chichester, states in his "Church Dictionary," under "Prayer," that "the general providence of God acts through what are called the laws of nature. By his particular providence, God interferes with those laws; and he has promised to interfere in behalf of those who pray in the name of Jesus. . . . We may take it as a general rule that we may pray for that for which we may lawfully labor, and for that only."

The phrases of our church service amply countenance this view; and, if we look to the practice of the opposed sections of the religious world, we find them consistent in maintaining it. The so-called "Low Church" notoriously places absolute belief in special providences accorded to pious prayer. This is testified by the biographies of its members, the journals of its missionaries, and the "united prayer-meetings" of the present day. The Roman Catholics offer religious vows to avert danger; they make pilgrimages to shrines; they hang votive offerings and pictorial representations, sometimes by thousands, in their churches, of fatal accidents averted by the manifest interference of a solicited saint.

A *primâ facie* argument in favor of the efficacy of prayer is therefore to be drawn from the very general use of it. The greater part of mankind, during all the historic ages, have been accustomed to pray for temporal advantages. How vain, it may be urged, must be the reasoning that ventures to oppose this mighty consensus of belief! Not so. The argument of universality either proves too much, or else it is suicidal. It either compels us to admit that the prayers of Pagans, of Fetish worshippers, and of Buddhists who turn praying-wheels, are recompensed in the same way as those of orthodox believers; or else the general consensus proves that it has no better foundation than the universal tendency of man to gross credulity.

The collapse of the argument of universality leaves us solely concerned with a simple statistical question, Are prayers answered, or are they not? There are two lines of research, by either of which we may pursue this inquiry. The one that promises the most trustworthy results is to examine large classes of cases, and to be guided by broad averages: the other, which I will not employ in these pages, is to deal with isolated instances. An author who made much use of the latter method might reasonably suspect his own judgment: he would certainly run the risk of being suspected by others in choosing one-sided examples.

The principles are broad and simple upon which our inquiry into the efficacy of prayer must be established. We must gather cases for statistical comparison, in which the same object is keenly pursued by two classes, — similar in their physical, but opposite in their spiritual state; the one class being prayerful, the other materialistic. Prudent pious people must be compared with prudent materialistic people, and not with the imprudent nor the vicious. Secondly, we have no regard, in this inquiry, to the course by which the answer to prayers may be supposed to operate. We simply look to the final result, — whether those who pray attain their objects more frequently than those who do not pray, but who live, in all other respects, under similar conditions. Let us now apply our principles to different cases.

A rapid recovery from disease may be conceived to depend on many causes besides the reparative power of the patient's constitution. A miraculous quelling of the disease may be one of these causes: another is the skill of the physician or of the nurse: another is the care that the patient takes of himself. In our inquiry, whether prayerful people recover more rapidly than others, under similar circumstances, we need not complicate the question by endeavoring to learn the channel through which the patient's prayer may have reached its fulfilment. It is foreign to our present purpose to ask if there be any signs of a miraculous quelling of the disease, or if, through the grace of God, the physician had showed unusual wisdom, or the nurse or the patient unusual discretion. We simply look to the main issue, — do sick persons who pray, or are prayed for, recover, on the average, more rapidly than others?

It appears, that, in all countries and in all creeds, the priests urge the patient to pray for his own recovery, and the patients' friends to aid him with their prayers, but that the doctors make no account whatever of their spiritual agencies, unless the office of priest and medical man be combined in the same individual. The medical works of modern Europe teem with records of individual illness and of broad averages of disease; but I have been able to discover hardly any instance in which a medical man of any repute has attributed recovery to the influence of prayer. There is not a single instance, to my knowledge, in which papers read before statistical societies have recognized the agency of prayer, either on disease or on any thing else. The universal habit of the scientific world to ignore the agency of prayer is a very important fact. To fully appreciate the "eloquence of the silence" of medical men, we must bear in mind the care with which they endeavor to assign a sanatory value to every influence. Had prayers for the sick any notable effect, it is incredible but that the doctors, who are always on the watch for such things, should have observed it, and added their influence to that of the priests towards obtaining them for every sick man. If they abstain from doing so, it is not because their attention has never been awakened to the possible efficacy of prayer, but, on the contrary, that, although they have heard it insisted on from childhood upwards, they are unable to detect its influence. Most people have some general belief in the objective efficacy of prayer; but none seem willing to admit its action in those special cases of which they have scientific cognizance.

Those who may wish to pursue these inquiries upon the effect of prayer for the restoration of health could obtain abundant materials from hospital cases, and in a different way from that proposed in the challenge to which I referred in the beginning of these pages. There are many common maladies whose course is so thoroughly well understood as to admit of accurate tables of probability being constructed for their duration and result. Such are fractures and amputations. Now, it would be perfectly practicable to select out of the patients at different hospitals, under treatment for fractures and amputations, two considerable groups,—the one consisting of markedly religious and piously befriended individuals, the other of those who were remarkably cold-hearted and neglected. An honest comparison of their respective periods of treatment, and the results, would manifest a distinct proof of the efficacy of prayer, if it existed, to even a minute fraction of the amount that religious teachers exhort us to believe.

An inquiry of a somewhat similar nature may be made

into the longevity of persons whose lives are prayed for, also that of the praying classes generally; and in both these cases we can easily obtain statistical facts. The public prayer for the sovereign of every state, Protestant or Catholic, is, and has been, in the spirit of our own, "Grant her in health long to live." Now, as a simple matter of fact, has this prayer any efficacy? There is a memoir by Dr. Guy, in "The Journal of the Statistical Society" (vol. xxii. p. 355), in which he compares the mean age of sovereigns with that of other classes of persons. His results are expressed in the following table: —

MEAN AGE ATTAINED BY MALES OF VARIOUS CLASSES WHO HAD SURVIVED THEIR THIRTIETH YEAR, FROM 1758 TO 1843. DEATHS BY ACCIDENT OR VIOLENCE ARE EXCLUDED.

	Number.	Average.	Eminent men.[1]
Members of royal houses	97	64.04	
Clergy	945	69.49	66.42
Lawyers	294	68.14	66.51
Medical profession	244	67.31	67.07
English aristocracy	1,179	67.31	
Gentry	1,632	70.22	
Trade and commerce	513	68.74	
Officers in the royal navy . . .	366	68.40	
English literature and science . .	395	67.55	65.22
Officers of the army	569	67.07	
Fine arts	239	65.96	64.74

The sovereigns are literally the shortest lived of all who have the advantage of affluence. The prayer has, therefore, no efficacy, unless the very questionable hypothesis be raised, that the conditions of royal life may naturally be yet more

[1] The eminent men are those whose lives are recorded in Chalmers's Biography, with some additions from the Annual Register.

fatal, and that their influence is partly, though incompletely, neutralized by the effect of public prayers.

It will be seen that the same table collates the longevity of clergy, lawyers, and medical men. We are justified in considering the clergy to be a far more prayerful class than either of the other two. It is their profession to pray; and they have the practice of offering morning and evening family prayers in addition to their private devotions. A reference to any of the numerous published collections of family prayers will show that they are full of petitions for temporal benefits. We do not, however, find that the clergy are in any way more long lived in consequence. It is true, that the clergy, as a whole, show a life-value of 69.49 as against 68.14 for the lawyers, and 67.31 for the medical men; but the easy country-life and family repose of so many of the clergy are obvious sanatory conditions in their favor. This difference is reversed when the comparison is made between distinguished members of the three classes; that is to say, between persons of sufficient note to have had their lives recorded in a biographical dictionary. When we examine this category, the value of life among the clergy, lawyers, and medical men, is as 66.42, 66.51, and 67.04 respectively; the clergy being the shortest lived of the three. Hence the prayers of the clergy for protection against the perils and dangers of the night, for protection during the day, and for recovery from sickness, appear to be futile in result.

In my work on "Hereditary Genius," and in the chapter on "Divines," I have worked out the subject with some minuteness on other data, but with precisely the same result. I show that the divines are not specially favored in those worldly matters for which they naturally pray, but rather the contrary, — a fact which I ascribe, in part, to their having, as a class, indifferent constitutional vigor. I give abundant reason for all this, and do not care to repeat myself; but I should be glad if such of the readers of this present paper who may be accustomed to statistics would refer to the chapter I have mentioned. They will find it of use in confirming what I say here. They will believe me the more when I say that I have taken considerable pains to get at the truth in the questions raised in this present memoir, and that, when I was engaged upon them, I worked, as far as my material went, with as much care as I gave to that chapter on "Divines;" and, lastly, they will understand, that, when writing the chapter in question, I had all this material by me unused, which justified me in speaking out as decidedly as I did then.

A further inquiry may be made into the duration of life among missionaries. We should lay greater stress upon their mortality than upon that of the clergy, because the laudable object of a missionary's career is rendered almost nugatory by his early death. A man goes, say, to a tropical climate, in the prime of manhood, who has the probability of many years of useful life before him, had he remained at home. He has the certainty of being able to accomplish sterling good as a missionary, if he should live long enough to learn the language and habits of the country. In the interval, he is almost useless. Yet the painful experience of many years shows only too clearly that the missionary is not supernaturally endowed with health. He does not live longer than other people. One missionary after another dies shortly after his arrival. The work that lay almost within the grasp of each of them lingers incompleted.

It must be here repeated, that comparative immunity from disease compels the suspension of no purely material law, if such an expression be permitted. Tropical fever, for example, is due to many subtle causes which are partly under man's control. A single hour's exposure to sun, wet, or fatigue, or mental agitation, will determine an attack. Now, even if God acted only on the minds of the missionaries, his action might be as much to the advantage of their health as if he wrought a physical miracle. He could disincline them to take those courses which might result in mischance, such as the forced march, the wetting, the abstinence from food, or the night-exposure, any one of which was competent to develop the fever that struck them down. We must not dwell upon the circumstances of individual cases, and say, "This was a providential escape," or, "That was a salutary chastisement:" but we must take the broad averages of mortality; and, when we do so, we find that the missionaries do not form a favored class.

The efficacy of prayer may yet further be tested by inquiry into the proportion of deaths at the time of birth among the children of the praying and the non-praying classes. The solicitude of parents is so powerfully directed toward the safety of their expected offspring, as to leave no room to doubt that pious parents pray fervently for it, especially as death before baptism is considered a most serious evil by many Christians. However, the distribution of still-births appears wholly unaffected by piety. The proportion, for instance, of the still-births published in "The Record" newspaper, and in "The Times, was found, by me, on an examination of a particular period, to bear an identical relation to the total number of deaths. This inquiry might easily be pursued by those who considered that more ample evidence was required.

When we pray in our Liturgy, "that the nobility may be endued with grace, wisdom, and understanding," we pray for that which is clearly incompatible with insanity. Does that frightful scourge spare our nobility? Does it spare very religious people more than others? The answer is an emphatic negative to both of these questions. The nobility — probably from their want of the wholesome restraints felt in the humble walks of life, and from their intermarriages — and the very religious people of all denominations — probably from their meditation on hell — are peculiarly subject to it. Religious madness is very common indeed.

As I have already hinted, I do not propose any special

inquiry whether the general laws of physical nature are ever suspended in fulfilment of prayer; whether, for instance, success has attended the occasional prayers in the Liturgy, when they have been used for rain, for fair weather, for the stilling of the sea in a storm, or for the abatement of a pestilence. I abstain from doing so for two reasons.

First, if it is proved that God does not answer one large class of prayers at all, it would be of less importance to pursue the inquiry. Secondly, the modern feeling of this country is so opposed to a belief in the occasional suspension of the general laws of nature, that an English reader would merely smile at such an investigation.

If we are satisfied that the actions of man are not influenced by prayer, even through the subtle influence of his thoughts and will, the only probable form of agency will have been disproved, and no one would care to advance a claim in favor of direct physical interferences.

Biographies do not show that devotional influences have clustered in any remarkable degree round the youth of those, who, whether by their talents or social position, have left a mark upon our English history. Lord Campbell, in his Preface to his "Lives of the Chancellors," says, "There is no office in the history of any nation that has been filled with such a long succession of distinguished and interesting men as the office of lord-chancellor," and that, "generally speaking, the most eminent men, if not the most virtuous, have been selected to adorn it." His implied disparagement of their piety is fully sustained by an examination of their respective biographies, and by a taunt of Horace Walpole, quoted in the same Preface. An equal absence of remarkable devotional tendencies may be observed in the lives of the leaders of great political parties. The founders of our great families too often owed their advancement to tricky and time-serving courtiership. The belief so frequently expressed in the Psalms, that the descendants of the righteous shall continue, and that those of the wicked shall surely fail, is not fulfilled in the history of our English peerage. Take, for instance, the highest class, that of the ducal houses. The influence of social position in this country is so enormous, that the possession of a dukedom is a power that can hardly be understood without some sort of calculation. There are, I believe, only twenty-seven dukes to about eight millions of adult male Englishmen, or about three dukes to each million; yet the cabinet of fourteen ministers which governs this country, and India too, commonly contains one duke, often two, and in recent times three. The political privilege inherited with a dukedom in this country is, at the lowest estimate, many thousand-fold above the average birthright of Englishmen. What was the origin of these ducal families, whose influence on the destiny of England and her dependencies is so enormous? Were their founders the eminently devout children of eminently pious parents? Have they and their ancestors been distinguished among the praying classes? Not so. I give in a footnote a list of their names,[1] which recalls many a deed of patriotism, valor, and skill, many an instance of eminent merit of the worldly sort, — which we Englishmen honor six days out of the seven, — many scandals, many a disgrace, but not, on the other hand, a single instance known to me of eminently prayerful qualities. Four, at least, of the existing ducal houses, are unable to claim the title of having been raised into existence through the devout habits of their progenitors, because the families of Buccleuch, Grafton, St. Albans, and Richmond, were thus highly ennobled solely on the ground of their being descended from Charles II. and four of his mistresses; namely, Lucy Walters, Barbara Villiers, Nell Gwynne, and Louise de Querouaille. The Dukedom of Cleveland may almost be reckoned as a fifth instance.

The civil liberty we enjoy in England, and the energy of our race, have given rise to a number of institutions, societies, commercial adventures, political meetings, and combinations of all sorts. Some of these are exclusively clerical, some lay, and others mixed. It is impossible for a person to have taken an active share in social life without having had abundant means of estimating for himself, and of hearing the opinion of others, on the value of a preponderating clerical element in business committees. For my own part,

[1] Abercorn, Argyll, Athole, Beaufort, Bedford, Buccleuch, Buckingham, Cleveland, Devonshire, Grafton, Hamilton, Leeds, Leinster, Manchester, Marlborough, Montrose, Newcastle, Norfolk, Northumberland, Portland, Richmond, Roxburghe, Rutland, St. Albans, Somerset, Sutherland, Wellington.

I never heard a favorable one. The procedure of convocation, which, like all exclusively clerical meetings, is opened with prayer, has not inspired the outer world with much respect. The histories of the great councils of the church are most painful to read. There is reason to expect that devout and superstitious men should be unreasonable; for a person who believes his thoughts to be inspired, necessarily accredits his prejudices with divine authority. He is, therefore, little accessible to argument, and he is intolerant of those whose opinions differ from his, especially on first principles. Consequently he is a bad coadjutor in business matters. It is a common week-day opinion of the world that praying people are not practical.

Again: there is a large class of instances, where an enterprise on behalf of pious people is executed by the agency of the profane. Do such enterprises prosper beyond the average? For instance, a vessel on a missionary errand is navigated by ordinary seamen. A fleet, followed by the prayers of the English nation, carries re-enforcements to quell an Indian mutiny. We do not care to ask whether the result of the prayers is to obtain favorable winds, but simply whether they ensue in a propitious voyage, whatever may have been the agencies by which that result was obtained. The success of voyages might be due to many other agencies than the suspension of the physical laws that control the winds and currents; just as we showed that a rapid recovery from illness might be due to other causes than direct interference with cosmic order. It might have been put into the captain's heart to navigate in that course, and to perform those acts of seamanship which proved links in a chain that led to an eventual success. A very small matter would suffice to make a great difference in the end. A vessel navigated by a man who was a good forecaster of weather, and an accomplished hydrographer, would considerably outstrip another that was deficient in so accomplished a commander, but otherwise similarly equipped. The perfectly instructed navigator would deviate from the most direct course by, perhaps, some mere trifle, first here, then there, in order to bring his vessel within favoring slants of wind and advantageous currents. A ship commanded by a captain, and steered by a sailor, whose hearts were miraculously acted upon in answer to prayer, would unconsciously, as by instinct, or even, as it were, by mistake, perform these deviations from routine, which would lead to ultimate success.

The missionaries who are the most earnestly prayed for are usually those who are on routes where there is little traffic, and therefore where there is more opportunity for the effects of secret providential overruling to display themselves than among those who sail in ordinary sea-voyages. In the usual sea-routes, a great deal is known of the peculiarities of the seasons and currents, and of the whereabouts of hidden dangers of all kinds: their average risk is small, and the insurance is low. But, when vessels are bound to ports like those sought by the missionaries, the case is different. The risk that attends their voyages is largely increased; and the insurance is proportionately raised. But is the risk equally increased in respect to missionary vessels, and to those of traders and of slave-dealers? The comparison between the fortune that attends prayerful and non-prayerful people may here be most happily made. The missionaries are eminently among the former category; and the slave-dealers and the traders we speak of, in the other. Traders in the unhealthy and barbarous regions to which we refer are notoriously the most godless and reckless (on the broad average) of any of their set. We have, unfortunately, little knowledge of the sea-risks of slavers, because the rates of their insurance involve the risk of capture. There is, however, a universal testimony, in the parliamentary reports on slavery, to the excellent and skilful manner in which these vessels are sailed and navigated, which is a *primâ facie* reason for believing their sea-risks to be small. As to the relative risks run by ordinary traders and missionary vessels, the insurance offices absolutely ignore the slightest difference between them. They look to the class of the vessel, and to the station to which she is bound, and to nothing else. The notion that a missionary or other pious enterprise carries any immunity from danger has never been entertained by insurance companies.

To proceed with our inquiry, whether enterprises in behalf of pious people succeed better than others when they are intrusted to profane hands, we may ask, Is a bank or other commercial undertaking more secure when devout men are among its shareholders, or when the funds of pious people, or charities, or of religious bodies, are deposited in its keeping, or when its proceedings are opened with prayer, as was the case with the disastrous Royal British Bank? It is impossible to say Yes. There are far too many sad experiences of the contrary. If prayerful habits had influence on temporal success, it is very probable, as we must again repeat, that insurance offices, of at least some descriptions, would long ago have discovered, and made allowance for it. It would be most unwise, from a business point of view, to allow the devout, supposing their greater longevity even probable, to obtain annuities at the same low rates as the profane. Before insurance companies accept a life, they make confidential inquiries into the antecedents of the applicant. But such a question has never been heard of as, "Does he habitually use family prayers and private devotions?" Insurance offices, so wakeful to sanatory influences, absolutely ignore prayer as one of them. The same is true for insurances of all descriptions, as those connected with fire, ships, lightning, hail, accidental death, and cattle-sickness. How is it possible to explain why Quakers, who are most devout and most shrewd men of business, have ignored these considerations, except on the ground that they do not really believe in what they and others freely assert about the efficacy of prayer? It was, at one time, considered an act of mistrust in an overruling Providence, to put lightning-conductors on churches; for it was said that God would surely take care of his own. But Arago's collection of the accidents from lightning showed they were sorely needed; and now lightning-conductors are universal. Other kinds of accidents befall churches equally with other buildings of the same class; such as architectural flaws (resulting in great expenses for repair), fires, earthquakes, and avalanches.

The cogency of all these arguments is materially increased by the recollection that many items of ancient faith have been successively abandoned by the Christian world to the domain of recognized superstition. It is not two centuries ago, long subsequent to the days of Shakspeare and other great names, that the sovereign of this country was accustomed to lay hands on the sick for their recovery, under the sanction of a regular church service, which was not omitted from our prayer-books till the time of George II. Witches were unanimously believed in, and were regularly exorcised, and punished by law, up to the beginning of the last century. Ordeals and duels, most reasonable solutions of complicated difficulties, according to the popular theory of religion, were found absolutely fallacious in practice. The miraculous power of relics and images, still so general in Southern Europe, is scouted in England. The importance ascribed to dreams, the barely extinct claims of astrology, and auguries of good or evil luck, and many other well-known products of superstition which are found to exist in every country, have ceased to be believed in by us. This is the natural course of events, just as the Waters of Jealousy, and the Urim and the Thummim of the Mosaic law, had become obsolete in the times of the later Jewish kings. The civilized world has already yielded an enormous amount of honest conviction to the inexorable requirements of honest fact; and it seems to me clear, that all belief in the efficacy of prayer, in the sense in which I have been considering it, must be yielded also. The evidence I have been able to collect bears wholly and solely in that direction; and, in the face of it, the *onus probandi* lies henceforth on the other side.

Nothing that I have said negatives the fact that the mind may be relieved by the utterance of prayer. The impulse to pour out the feelings in sound is not peculiar to man. Any mother that has lost her young, and wanders about, moaning, and looking piteously for sympathy, possesses much of that which prompts men to pray in articulate words. There is a yearning of the heart, a craving for help, it knows not where, certainly from no source that it sees. Of a similar kind is the bitter cry of the hare when the greyhound is almost upon her: she abandons hope through her own efforts, and screams — but to whom? It is a voice convulsively sent out into space, whose utterance is a physical relief. These feelings of distress and of terror are simple; and an inarticulate cry suffices to give vent to them. But the reason why man is not satisfied by uttering inarticulate cries (though sometimes they are felt to be the most appropriate) is owing to his superior intellectual powers. His memory travels back through interlacing paths, and dwells on various connected incidents: his emotions are complex; and he prays at length.

Neither does any thing I have said profess to throw light on the question of how far it is possible for man to commune in his heart with God. We know that many persons of high intellectual gifts and critical minds look upon it as an axiomatic certainty that they possess this power, although it is impossible for them to establish any satisfactory criterion to distinguish between what may really be borne in upon them from without, and what arises from within, but which, through a sham of the imagination, appears to be external. A confident sense of communion with God must necessarily rejoice and strengthen the heart, and divert it from petty cares; and it is equally certain that similar benefits are not excluded from those, who, on conscientious grounds, are sceptical as to the reality of a power of communion. These can dwell on the undoubted fact that there exists a solidarity between themselves and what surrounds them, through the endless re-actions of physical laws, among which the hereditary influences are to be included. They know that they are descended from an endless past, that they have a brotherhood with all that is, and have each his own share of responsibility in the parentage of an endless future. The effort to familiarize the imagination with this great idea has much in common with the effort of communing with a God; and its re-action on the mind of the thinker is, in many important respects, the same. It may not equally rejoice the heart; but it is quite as powerful in ennobling the resolves; and it is found to give serenity during the trials of life, and in the shadow of approaching death.

FRANCIS GALTON.

V.

ON PRAYER.

1.—BY PROFESSOR TYNDALL.

2.—BY THE AUTHOR OF "HINTS TOWARDS A SERIOUS ATTEMPT TO ESTIMATE THE VALUE OF THE 'PRAYER FOR THE SICK.'"

3.—BY JAMES McCOSH, D.D., PRESIDENT OF PRINCETON COLLEGE, UNITED STATES.

THESE three papers appeared in this order in "The Contemporary Review," October, 1872. In the first, Mr. Tyndall suggests his own views, which were not set forth in his brief Introductory Note to the original "Hints," &c., though his views might be inferred. The author of "The Hints," in this second paper, replies to Dr. Littledale, and re-enforces the argument of his original communication. Dr. McCosh's paper was intended as an answer to the original communications of Mr. Tyndall and his friend, and did not have reference to their replies, published in the same number of the review which contained Dr. McCosh's Defence of Prayer.

V.

ON PRAYER.

1.

THE editor of "The Contemporary Review" is liberal enough to grant me space for a few brief reflections on a subject, a former reference to which, in these pages, has, I believe, brought down upon me a considerable amount of animadversion.

It may be interesting to some, if I glance at a few cases illustrative of the history of the human mind in relation to this and kindred subjects. In the fourth century, the belief in antipodes was deemed unscriptural and heretical. The pious Lactantius was as angry with the people who held this notion as my censors are with me, and quite as unsparing in his denunciations of their "monstrosities." Lactantius was irritated, because, in his mind, by education and habit, cosmogony and religion were indissolubly associated, and therefore simultaneously disturbed. In the early part of the seventeenth century, the notion that the earth was fixed, and that the sun and stars revolved round it daily, was interwoven in a similar manner with religious feeling; the separation then attempted by Galileo arousing animosity, and kindling persecution. Men still living can remember the indignation excited by the first revelations of geology, regarding the age of the earth; the association between chronology and religion being for the time indissoluble. In our day, however, the best-informed clergymen are prepared to admit that our views of the universe and its Author are not impaired, but improved, by the abandonment of the Mosaic account of the creation. Look, finally, at the excitement caused by the publication of "The Origin of Species," and compare it with the calm attendant on the appearance of the far more outspoken, and, from the old point of view, more impious, "Descent of Man."

Thus religion survives after the removal of what had been long considered essential to it. In our day the antipodes are accepted; the fixity of the earth is given up; the period of creation, and the reputed age of the world, are alike dissipated; evolution is looked upon without terror; and other changes have occurred in the same direction too numerous to be dwelt upon here. In fact, from the earliest times to the present, religion has been undergoing a process of purification, freeing itself slowly and painfully from the physical errors which the busy and uninformed intellect mingled with the aspiration of the soul, and which ignorance sought to perpetuate. Some of us think a final act of purification remains to be performed; while others oppose this notion with the confidence and the warmth of ancient times. The bone of contention, at present, is *the physical value of prayer.* It is not my wish to excite surprise, much less to draw forth protest, by the employment of this phrase. I would simply ask any intelligent person to look the problem honestly and steadily in the face, and then to say whether, in the estimation of the great body of those who sincerely resort to it, prayer does not, at all events upon special occasions, invoke a Power which checks and augments the descent of rain, which changes the force and direction of winds, which affects the growth of corn, and the health of men and cattle, — a Power, in short, which, when appealed to under pressing circumstances, produces the precise effects caused by physical energy in the ordinary course of things. To any person who deals sincerely with the subject, and refuses to blur his moral vision by intellectual subtleties, this, I think, will appear a true statement of the case.

It is under this aspect alone that the scientific student, so far as I represent him, has any wish to meddle with prayer. Forced upon his attention as a form of physical energy, or as the equivalent of such energy, he claims the right of subjecting it to those methods of examination from which all our present knowledge of the physical universe is derived. And if his researches lead him to a conclusion adverse to its claims; if his inquiries rivet him still closer to the philosophy infolded in the words, "He maketh his sun to shine on the evil and on the good, and sendeth rain upon the just and upon the unjust," — he contends only for the displacement of prayer, not for its extinction. He simply says, physical nature is not its legitimate domain.

This conclusion, moreover, must be based on pure physical evidence, and not on any inherent unreasonableness in the act of prayer. The theory that the system of nature is under the control of a Being who changes phenomena in compliance with the prayers of men, is, in my opinion, a perfectly legitimate one. It may, of course, be rendered futile by being associated with conceptions which contradict it; but such conceptions form no necessary part of the theory. It is a matter of experience that an earthly father, who is at the same time both wise and tender, listens to the requests of his children, and, if they do not ask amiss, takes pleasure in granting their requests. We know, also, that this compliance extends to the alteration, within certain limits, of the current of events on earth. With this suggestion offered by our experience, it is no departure from scientific method to place behind natural phenomena a universal Father, who, in answer to the prayers of his children, alters the currents of those phenomena. Thus far, theology and science go hand in hand. The conception of an ether, for example, trembling with the waves of light, is suggested by the ordinary phenomena of wave-motion in water and in air; and, in like manner, the conception of personal volition in nature is suggested by the ordinary action of man upon earth. I therefore urge no *impossibilities*, though you constantly charge me with doing so. I do not even urge inconsistency, but, on the contrary, frankly admit that you have as good a right to place your conception at the root of phenomena as I have to place mine.

But, without *verification*, a theoretic conception is a mere figment of the intellect; and I am sorry to find us parting company at this point. The region of theory, both in science and theology, lies behind the world of the senses; but the verification of theory occurs in the sensible world. To check the theory, we have simply to compare the deductions from it with the facts of observation. If the deductions be in accordance with the facts, we accept the theory: if in opposition, the theory is given up. A single experiment is frequently devised by which the theory must stand or fall. Of this character was the determination of the velocity of light in liquids as a crucial test of the Emission Theory. According to Newton, light travelled faster in water than in air: according to an experiment suggested by Arago, and executed by Fizeau and Foucault, it travelled faster in air than in water. The experiment was conclusive against Newton's theory.

But, while science cheerfully submits to this ordeal, it seems impossible to devise a mode of verification of their theory which does not arouse resentment in theological minds. Is it, that, while the pleasure of the scientific man culminates in the demonstrated harmony between theory and fact, the highest pleasure of the religious man has been already tasted in the very act of praying, prior to verification; any further effort in this direction being a mere disturbance of his peace? Or is it that we have before us a residue of that mysticism of the middle ages which has been so admirably described by Whewell, — that "practice of referring things and events, not to clear and distinct notions, not to general rules capable of direct verification, but to notions vague, distant, and vast, which we cannot bring into contact with facts, as when we connect natural events with moral and historic causes"? "Thus," he continues, "the character of mysticism is, that it refers particulars, not to generalizations homogeneous and immediate, but to such as are heterogeneous and remote;" to which we must add, that the process of this reference is not a calm act of the intellect, but is accompanied with a glow of enthusiastic feeling.

Every feature here depicted, and some more questionable ones, have shown themselves of late most conspicuously, I regret to say, in the "leaders" of a weekly journal of considerable influence, and one on many grounds entitled to the respect of thoughtful men. In the correspondence, however, published by the same journal, are to be found two or three letters well calculated to correct the temporary flightiness of the journal itself.

It is not my habit of mind to think otherwise than solemnly of the feeling which prompts prayer. It is a potency which I should like to see guided, not extinguished, devoted to practicable objects, instead of wasted upon air. In some form or other, not yet evident, it may, as alleged, be necessary to man's highest culture. Certain it is, that, while I rank many persons who employ it low in the scale of being,—natural foolishness, bigotry, and intolerance being, in their case, intensified by the notion that they have access to the ear of God,—I regard others who employ it as forming part of the very cream of the earth. The faith that simply adds to the folly and ferocity of the one is turned to enduring sweetness, holiness, abounding charity, and self-sacrifice by the other. Christianity, in fact, varies with the nature upon which it falls. Often unreasonable, if not contemptible, in its purer forms prayer hints at disciplines which few of us can neglect without moral loss. But no good can come of giving it a delusive value, by claiming for it a power in physical nature. It may strengthen the heart to meet life's losses, and thus indirectly promote physical well-being, as the digging of Æsop's orchard brought a treasure of fertility greater than the treasure sought. Such indirect issues we all admit; but it would be simply dishonest to affirm that it is such issues that are always in view. Here, for the present, I must end. I ask no space to reply to those railers who make such free use of the terms "insolence," "outrage," "profanity," and "blasphemy." They obviously lack the sobriety of mind necessary to give accuracy to their statements, or to render their charges worthy of serious refutation.

John Tyndall.

2.

In a paper published in "The Contemporary Review" of July last, I made a proposal to ascertain, by a practical test, the value of prayer on behalf of the sick. It was my aim to invite the attention of all thoughtful persons; but I desired co-operation especially from those who have a firm belief in the value of such prayer. Strange to say, none of the latter have responded in a favorable sense. Indeed, by many my proposal has been called "profane," "irreligious," and by other similar epithets; while, in the numerous articles which have appeared on the subject, I myself have been termed "materialist" and "infidel," whatever those appellations may signify. Nevertheless, I have often observed invitations to united prayer issued for various objects to the "religious world," — such as for the prosperity of Sunday schools, the conversion of the Jews or of foreign peoples to Christianity, — and that the invitations have been largely and devoutly complied with. In the last-named instance, I have read glowing descriptions of the obvious answers that have been vouchsafed to such prayer; and I have even seen numerical estimates of the conversions which have thus been effected. Yet, and with equal solemnity, I have said to the religious world, "Let us pray;" and the religious world has declined the exercise. This strikes me as a remarkable circumstance; and I propose to inquire why it has occurred; for the object of prayer — the recovery of the sick — is, as I have formerly shown, universally admitted by the Christian Church to be a legitimate one. And the ultimate aim of my proposal was, that the value of prayer might be not only estimated, but also utilized, to a larger extent than heretofore, on behalf, at any rate, of our great charitable institutions. What was there in this to warrant the opposition, the abuse, the attempt to affix the *odium theologicum*, which the proposal encounters? Why, indeed, was my suggestion not regarded with favor by professedly religious people, and embraced with that activity and fervor which would certainly have been manifested by many, had I proposed special services for the conversion of the "heathen," instead of for the recovery of the sick? I propose, at the outset, to pursue this inquiry.

Some things seem to have been wholly lost sight of, or not understood, by my opponents. Among these, I must include the Rev. R. F. Littledale, whose paper on "The Rationale of Prayer" appeared in the August number, so far as he criticises my proposal, although the article mainly applies to Prof. Tyndall.

Now, at the outset, that which strikes me most forcibly, and, I must confess, which painfully shocks me, is the extreme ignorance of what is comprehended by the exercise, — prayer, — and the really irreligious state of heart, if I may borrow what is almost a theological metaphor, manifested by my critics, especially those who write from the *soi-disant* "religious" side of the question. For example, while I specifically designed an inquiry to ascertain the value of "prayer for the sick," and by means of this the value of direct petition for material benefits of any kind, as classified by me, I am charged with denying directly, or by implication, the value of prayer altogether? It scarcely seems to enter into the schemes of my opponents, that to some minds, especially may I say to the minds of the much abused physicist, the larger and more important part of prayer is that which is in no sense of the words a petitioning for benefits. Dr. Littledale, in replying to Prof. Tyndall's obvious allusion to this larger sense (in a passage quoted), denies that it has that meaning, and terms the secondary or reflected benefit arising to the mind from prayer for good, to which he limits it, "an immoral sham;" "is at a loss to guess what kind of a God he" [the professor] "is willing to pray to, or what kind of blessings he is prepared to pray for." Mark, —"blessings to pray for,"—always petition, and, beyond petition, nothing! Prof. Tyndall can well take care of himself; and I shall interfere in no part of the question between himself and Dr. Littledale, except so far as it concerns views which I myself hold. Besides, I have not the least means of knowing what the belief of Prof. Tyndall may be, except through his writings, having but once spoken to him on the subject of my former paper, and having had no sort of communication with him of any kind since. I am compelled to say this, lest he may be held answerable for any opinion of mine, except so far as his note of July last indicated. If prayer be nothing more than asking a Deity to confer, as gifts, many things which to our little vision and narrow circles of observing appear desirable, then I for one, in common with many other "physicists," have long labored under a delusion; and one of the nobler effects of prayer, I learn from the lips of a divine to be little better than "a fit of voluntary hysterics," — a condition, let me observe, twice applied to his opponents in the course of one article, I think I may fairly say with as little of real meaning as of good taste. However, I am willing to believe he is unacquainted with the malady.

I can understand how, in this practical and material age as it has become the fashion to call it, the great bulk of mankind has come to associate the idea of acquiring good, and that idea only, with the exercise of prayer. To ask that God may protect us in danger; that a carriage may convey us safely; that a medicine may be blessed, and so help us to get to our business again; that the rain may fall in the fields about us, when the crops are taking harm for want of water, — is the natural outcome of a man whose great aim in life (no doubt a legitimate aim) is to better himself. And it is very, very much in accord with the needs of an increasing population, when that aim becomes, perhaps, more difficult than ever of attainment. It is deemed nobler to ask for a clearer intellect, for greater self-control, and a mastery over passions; a not less material good each one, after all, and not less valuable in pursuing the aim described; computable, therefore, as pecuniary values, equally with the preceding goods, if need be, but by a more complex process. All such prayer springs from the instinct of self-preservation, of selfishness if you please. But, if this be the common faith, the common people have not been left to arrive at it by that road alone. Their religious teachers have through all time inculcated the self-seeking petition as a duty, and have called it "prayer." Perhaps no religious office has been more extolled, or more regarded as essential to religious life. And their teachers, especially those of the ancient church, have derived large revenues from its exercise by way of petition, especially for the preservation from suffering in a future state, of individuals who have been able to pay largely for the influence so exercised with the Deity. I observe that Dr. Littledale is evidently favorable to the exercise of this function.

But, since prayer has thus been so largely regarded and utilized as a means of augmenting wealth and comfort, I and others can scarcely be deemed irreligious, because, although very willing to accept these goods, we are compelled to doubt the value of the means employed for obtaining them. Moreover, it is greatly disappointing at first, to the matured man, to be thus forced to question it, having believed it implicitly by force of education when a youth. Indeed, the sincere, honest doubt can scarcely arise, except in a devout mind, — in a mind earnestly desirous to find the truth, and to accept it, however painful it may at first sight appear. The cessation to believe in the value of petition to the Most High is, at all events, an acknowledgment of a power lost, — a thing which all men part with reluctantly. The merely indifferent man, caring for none of these questions, will, if he think at all, exercise a worldly common-sense, and say, "All the world prays: what all the world has done must be right. If there be any value in prayer (petition), why should I deprive myself of it?" And, behold, he prayeth! — after his fashion. Now, "all the world prays," in that man's mouth, is as good reasoning as Dr. Littledale's, when he argues for the value of prayer from its universality. I shall presently consider the question of its practice throughout the world, and of the efficacy of prayer by way of petition, but will first endeavor to show what prayer may be according to the views of a physicist, and which, in all the criticisms I have read, never seems to be so much as dreamed of. Hence my painful sense of the want of real religious feeling outside the circle said to be so exclusive, and incapable of any lofty conceptions, or of any aims, indeed, beyond purely scientific investigation.

I am a physiologist, say, belonging to a section of the "narrow" physicists, or a geologist. I am engaged in a search after the manner or nature of work exercised by some great Power infinitely beyond me. What wonder and admiration overwhelm me as I trace the operation of a Supreme Intelligence! I may or may not anthropomorphize that

Power, and call "Him" "Creator," "Deity," "Father," what you will, — terms all equally good, but alike inadequate to imply the object or source of that inexpressible sense of admiration which fills me; each term feeble enough, and but slightly differing one from the other, in presence of the All Supreme, and in the act of tracing the symbols of originating Mind in the happily untranslatable text which occupies the patient and humble seeker after fact; an original, revealing beauty beyond imagining, power, resource, and order of the grandest kind; an unerring order, which in our experience knows no exception, is all-sufficient, and furnishes to us, its children, the highest type and model of perfect organization. Do I quail before the inexorable decree, the "necessity" of that order, if you please? Or may I not, rather, rejoice in it, confide, hope, trust in it, know that my own place is a part of the grand whole, and do my work unquestioningly and unsuggestingly? There is no influence so soothing, none so reconciling to the checkered conditions of life, as consciousness of the absolute stability of the Rock on which the physicist takes his stand, who, knowing the intelligent order that pervades the universe, believes in it, and, with true filial piety, would never suggest a petition for a change in the Great Will as touching any childish whim of his own. I cannot express my repugnance at the notion that supreme Intelligence and Wisdom can be influenced by the suggestion of any human mind, however great.

It is thus that we may breathe the true spirit of communion with the Unseen, here realize a sense of dependence upon that which is too great to be moved, and gladly cherish submission to the only Mastership found to be unchanging and sufficing. Here the physicist fears no catastrophe, regards calmly all that happens, whatever it may be, as the outcome of the forces that exist. His work, and the work of all men, the only work that satisfies and endures, is the finding and maintaining of truth, so far as he knows it, freely, giving equal license to every other man to do the same; comparing, as we do at this moment, our observations and experience, and, in the clash of thought, evoking truth, victory for whichever side matters not to him, since it surely will in the end be for the side of truth. For the future, he has no anxiety: the supreme Order in which he has a place and work cannot fail to provide; and he submits, without suggesting limits or a definition to the plan he never could have devised, and cannot compass, too glad to believe that all such Order is not to be influenced by human interference.

Such a spirit enters into a man's life, is part of it, needs no special seasons or excitement to evoke it: it is in him, burning spontaneously, and is not added from without by any "means of grace." Such is the devotion of the physicist; and the work of such a life is a perpetual prayer, an identification and communion of the worker with the spring of all force and power. Doubtless Luther felt this when he uttered his famous "laborâsse est orâsse." It may or may not be the spirit of Christianity according to the Church; but it is founded in truth. Is it not the realization and final consummation of all prayer, even of all petition, — last arrived at in man's course, — culmination of all matured piety expressed in the memorable ejaculation, "Thy will be done"?

But I am told that the profanity of my proposal consists in its object, inasmuch as this was not the recovery of the sick, but an endeavor to estimate by figures — that is, scientifically; that is, truly, nothing more — the value of petition on their behalf. And I am gravely told that the Most High would never answer prayer with such an end in view.

Oh, little estimate of the Supreme! My mind revolts against the tiny finite who thus seeks to measure by its own frail and irritable temper the quality of the Infinite. Are his thoughts as our thoughts, or his ways as our ways? Shall prayer, which at least is unselfish, and aims only at attaining truth, be so hardly dealt with on high? Has it not an aim as noble as the prayer that an army may be successful in killing, or that our people may amass greater wealth? Far be it from me to prescribe a limit to Almighty Will and Power and Goodness, to presume to assert how human motives are weighed by Supreme Wisdom! I could judge, no doubt, as to the result, were a narrow human mind to rule the universe, if such an intolerable idea be not too shocking. I do not think a great benevolent human ruler, a more than father to his creatures, would refuse to show what power his children might obtain by asking, supposing that he had repeatedly exhorted them to ask, and had promised to give liberally to all. In making such a supposition, I do but follow my opponents' cue, and have no intention of lowering my ideal of a Supreme Power to any likeness of any thing in earth or sky. Only, on their own showing, I contend that my critics are not warranted in denying that a good Deity would probably regard with favor my request. I quite understand, that, with the mental and moral constitution often attributed to Deity, some sense of affront to his personal dignity might perhaps be imagined by some men to stand in the way of the divine compliance. That is evidently the notion intended. Is it more ridiculous, or is it more painful, to learn that to such a miserable and primitive type the idea of God has descended, and that in a nation which vaunts itself not "heathen"?

The question comes home to me very forcibly, more so than it ever did before, Do these people believe in the efficacy of petition? Does the religious world really believe that the Sunday services affect the health, the wealth, the wisdom, of the prayed-for, diminish the deaths, increase the products of the field, preserve from accidents, &c.? Do they think, that, without such prayers, there would be more deaths and smaller crops? It either is or is not so; and no discussion about direct and indirect influence will avail one jot to obscure the question. Is the world to go on forever with such a problem unsolved? Will men be much longer content to be uncertain how far all the phenomena of life and its surroundings are obedient to perfect order, and are regulated by supreme wisdom, or how far they are influenced by the infinitely small and ignorant?

I know it will be retorted that Divine Wisdom selects the petitions, and answers only such as are wise and good; that is, such as are in perfect accord with itself, so that none need fear any undue meddling with the universal order. Why, then, petition? If all is to be left to Infinite Wisdom, after all, why make certainly ignorant, perhaps impertinent, suggestions? And who are they, even with "the gift of prayer" who shall ask in perfect harmony with the divine thought?

But suppose some wise, what is the highest wisdom attainable here in relation to that which rules the mighty scheme? To a physicist, less than nothing and vanity. He who most studies, most endeavors to search, who, laboring ever on the verge of the unknown, meekly, patiently, earnestly tries to press forward the slowly advancing realm of the known into the infinity of the dark unknown, will be the most ready to confess his ignorance, and will never presume to carry it, in the form of any petition for interference, into the court of the Most High. He knows but one desire, the prayer for "more light;" but he knows, too, that he must achieve his end by untiring labor; and that no light ever entered this world, within human experience, except in reward to much labor. And so, again, "laborare est orare."

Thus much for two of the chief grounds for non-compliance on the part of the religious world with my proposal, — their inadequate conceptions respecting prayer itself, and, secondly, their views of what it is reasonable to suppose might be the relations of a great, wise, and good Deity with his creatures.

I now desire briefly to show why it is difficult to believe that events are affected by petition to a Supreme Power; such as, for example, the recovery of the sick, the improvement of the weather, the health and wealth of particular persons, the preservation from murder and sudden death, &c. I may confess that my own very grave doubts on this question impelled me to propose a test. Dr. Littledale, in referring to the test, makes the following remark, with which I entirely agree, and which might have formed a motto (had it then been written) for my former paper; and how it is applicable to me in any sense of admonition, I am at a loss to conceive.

"A really scientific temper would say, 'The fact of the existence of this phenomenon' [the habit of prayer] 'entitles it to respectful consideration: the fact that all inquiry in lower spheres of knowledge testifies to the truth of normal sequence, perhaps of law, makes it antecedently probable that prayer also belongs to a sphere of law, and has a definite purpose in the economy of the universe; since, if it had no such purpose, it would not and could not exist at all. Therefore, instead of irrationally denying its efficacy, let us examine its practical operation, without insisting on deductively accommodating it to a preconceived hypothesis.'"

Is this not precisely what I proposed to do?

He adds another remark to the same purpose, which to most readers would seem almost profane; and, had I uttered it, what a torrent of abuse would have been called forth, and deservedly so! for I should have been guilty of using language, which, however just, would have been unjustifiable in me, because it would do unnecessary violence to the best sentiments and the religious feelings of many excellent people. I refer to the following: "For I can see no reason why prayer as an actual fact in the universe should not be investigated as patiently and exhaustively as tobacco" Somehow, from the pen of the Rev. Dr. Littledale, these words excite no criticism.

I believe that I may safely assume that all will agree, that certain events within everybody's knowledge have always happened with such absolute regularity, that no one would dream of petitioning Heaven for any change in their modes of occurrence, — events the order of which has never been disturbed during the historic period. Let me instance the rising and setting of the sun, the movements of the tide, the decay and death of all organized bodies: many more will suggest themselves to every mind. It is quite beside the mark to enter upon any metaphysical discussion of the terms "law," "order," "relation of cause to effect," and so forth. It suffices for our purpose that no sane and moderately intelligent person would dream of praying that the sun may appear on the morrow an hour sooner or later than his appointed time, that the action of the tide may be suspended or reversed, or that decay and consequent death may not take place in any given case. People pray for prolongation of life, or postponement of death; but no one thinks of asking that the event may never arrive. Why is this? And why does the practice of not praying for such things obtain among those who believe in the efficacy of petition for, let us call them, smaller matters? Simply because the person praying has an absolute conviction that the events in question are so fixed, unaltering, and unalterable, that they are beyond the scope of prayer. So we see that practically, and beyond all dispute, the phenomena of the universe are ranged by people who fully believe in the efficacy of petition in two categories, — a class, which I shall call number one, respecting which it is quite useless, if not presumptuous, to pray; and a class (number two) of events which are the legitimate objects of prayer. Now, it is curious to observe that there is no agreement at all among religious people as to the principles on which such classification is to be made. Some persons will place a much larger proportion of subjects in class one than others will, and *vice versa*. Had the objects which can be influenced by prayer been authoritatively defined, and particularly the objects specified which cannot be so influenced, a useful work for the Church would have been accomplished. For, without such guidance, many people must (from ignorance) be asking God for things which are unattainable in this manner; while others are not asking for good which might be so procured. In first examining this question, I called the Book of Common Prayer to my aid; and, although I found by inference some little indication of an answer there, it is by no means a satisfactory or complete one. The common-sense, shall I say, of some people, or the more precise intelligence of others, leads them to regard some objects as certainly not to be attained by petition. Thus, one of my opponents says, "Of course, it would be useless to pray for recovery in the case of hydrophobia," although he thinks that less severe maladies might be much modified through the influence of prayer. I notice this, because the idea is a typical one, and embodies the practice of a great number who might still hesitate so plainly to express in words their real belief. They summon Almighty Power when the requirement is not considerable; but when, as in the case of a formidable disease above quoted, the power of medicine appears to be *nil*, they have little or no hope from an appeal to Omnipotence.

But if the theory be true, that petition to the Deity is an available power to influence human events, then the line of demarcation referred to must absolutely exist. There is no escape from this inference. It is either right and reasonable to pray for an alteration of the earth's course round the sun, or it is not. There must be a category of events not affected by prayer; and there should be a category of events, if my opponents are right, which can be so affected. Now, I contend they are bound to define these categories. They are bound to say what may be prayed for, and what must not be prayed for. I offered to aid in the inquiry by a practical test, — a test which I am still quite ready to prove to be practicable, if necessary, in spite of all that has been said against it, and of the objections to it, which, it is rightly stated, I have myself foreseen. If they concede, as they must, that the alteration of a star's or of a planet's course is not a fit object of petition, the *onus probandi* of explaining why, and also of stating what objects may be prayed for, rests with them. If they consent to make *every* event a legitimate object of prayer, then they are released from this obligation, and not otherwise.

But what has been the practical mode of arranging the two classes hitherto? for that they have been recognized by religious people in all time, although perhaps almost unconsciously, is obvious. The comprehensiveness of either class has varied at different periods, but precisely in obedience to the intelligent acquaintance of mankind with physical phenomena, nothing more: there is the whole secret. In the early stages of man's history, when his acquaintance with those phenomena was far more intelligent, he was ready to make almost any event the object of petition to some imaginary unseen power, to any deity, or the many deities by which he fancied himself to be surrounded, — deities, be it remarked, of a malevolent or adverse character towards him; a belief natural enough to a man surrounded by the forces of Nature, which, as yet, he could not tame, or teach to do his bidding.

This dilemma, however, soon called forth an intermediate man, who obtained his share of food and shelter without labor, by claiming to possess some influence with the deity to be propitiated, or coaxed into compliance. Naturally, any occurrence might then furnish an object of petition; the credulity and ignorance of the worshipper, and the daring and tact of the intermediate man, being the two factors from which almost any absurdity was producible. From that time to the present, advance in knowledge has enlarged the class of objects not to be prayed for, and has also, by equal steps, diminished the pretensions of the intermediate man, producing, in his place, the priest, now an educated and conscientious teacher. It is not marvellous, however, that he is always in antagonism with the physicist. For it is solely due to the observation, labor, and thought of the patient searcher into the physical conditions of the universe, that, year by year during the world's history, its phenomena have been removed from the realm of the providential and supernatural, and placed in that of natural and unvarying order. Thus it is that Class I. grows larger day by day, while Class II. diminishes in like proportion. Where shall this progress stop? Will any say it stops to-day, or a year hence, or that it will not continue to go on as long as one single intelligent scientific worker dwells on the globe? Class I. must inevitably grow larger and larger; Class II., as inevitably smaller. When and where will the professed believer in petition venture to draw the line between them? He must follow, drawn by inexorable power, in the wake of advancing science, and after hard resistance, as always; giving up one post after another, and resigning event after event, to be detached from the once great class of objects to be prayed for, and admitting their title of admission into the great class of settled and ordered events not to be influenced by human interference, and capitulating with the best grace he may when forced to surrender.

So it follows, that what a man will pray for depends precisely on the extent of his intelligent acquaintance with the phenomena around and within him. The more ignorant he is of these, and of their modes of occurrence, the larger his field for petition: the more intelligent, the smaller must be his range.

Past experience, then, makes it very probable that the class of phenomena which have an order as defined as that of the movements of the heavenly bodies, that is, a regularity without known exception, is a very large one. And there are many, who, perhaps not unreasonably, believe the analogy thus offered to be so strong, that it is not improbable that there really are no events which are not equally determined by natural order, and might be equally foreseen and forecast, were we in possession of the necessary data.

To apply, by some means, a scientific method to solve a part of the problem, was the sole object of my proposal. It is matter of extreme satisfaction to me to find an authority so respected as that of Dr. Littledale agreeing with me on the legitimacy of the object, and asserting that the efficacy of petition to Deity is a subject for uncompromising, exhaustive scientific research. We differ as to the mode, — the devotion of the hospital ward to the purpose. That is a mere trifle: I simply desired to raise the question, and to call public attention to it. For a large majority of writers on this subject have labored to show that prayer is not a fit subject for such an inquiry, and that I have sinned by laying a profane hand on the ark of God, in proposing to learn whether or no he will thus specifically aid us in the humane work of battling with disease, suffering, and death. Still I am no partisan of the scheme, and shall gladly listen to a plan which shall better attain our common end. For myself, I take leave of the controversy. The practical work of life, which circumstances have laid on me, forbids my further participation at present in the inquiry. It is evidently full of interest for myriads of others also. As a contribution towards its solution, it is impossible to overrate Mr. Galton's laborious and scientific record relating to the subject, nor to overlook its importance. Had I done nothing more than elicit the production of this last work of his, I should have been amply content.

I have only to remind my former critics and any future ones, that it is beside the issue to term me or my views "materialistic," "fatalist," or the like. It forms no part of a candid reply to do so. And although many good people still respond to the prejudice so easily and so cheaply aroused by attaching epithets[1] which have little meaning, and are really designed to be opprobrious, the great body of the public desire a rational solution of every important question, and have a right to expect its discussion unalloyed with adventitious matter of this kind.

THE AUTHOR OF "HINTS TOWARDS A SERIOUS ATTEMPT TO ESTIMATE THE VALUE OF THE PRAYER FOR THE SICK."

ATHENÆUM CLUB, September, 1872.

3.

THERE is a story told somewhere, that, when Copernicus divulged his theory of the earth running round the sun, a countryman came to him, declaring that he would believe it when he saw it, and insisted on his working an experiment to give him ocular demonstration. I forget what Copernicus did; but I know that Francis Bacon would have said, "A man cannot enter the kingdom of nature in any other way than he enters the kingdom of heaven, — by becoming a little child," and by submitting to what the Master teaches, and the rules of his school.

The experiment proposed in the paper forwarded by Prof.

1 Even Dr. Littledale, with all his desire to test scientifically the value of prayer, condescends to style me "a materialistic surgeon or physician," for proposing a method, and adroitly contrives to associate me in the same paragraph with Voltaire. For what end, but to cause prejudice? surely not to enforce an argument.

Tyndall is not conceived in the spirit of Bacon. Every one sees how unreasonable it would be to propose, as a test of the efficacy of prayer, that all the clergy of the Church, joined by all the Dissenting ministers, should agree to pray that the sun should stand still on a certain day at noon, and to allow that prayer is of no value, provided he went on in his course. We laugh at Rousseau's method of settling the question of the existence of God: he was to pray, and then throw a stone at a tree, and decide in the affirmative or negative, according as it did, or did not, strike the object. The experiment projected by Prof. Tyndall's friend is scarcely less irrational.

A man has to enter the one kingdom as he does the other, — by a docile attention to its laws. But the laws of the two kingdoms are not the same. In the one, the investigator must patiently watch phenomena, and settle every thing by observation and experiment. But he would not thereby be required to submit to such a proposal as that made to Copernicus. The Christian has also a method which he follows; and he can explain it to those who may wish to follow it, and he can give good reasons for his belief in Providence and prayer. But he gets his evidence in a different way from the man of science; and he is not obliged, in logical consistency, to test his belief in the way propounded in the paper inserted in "The Contemporary Review."

(1.) The proposal is not consistent with the method and laws of God's spiritual kingdom. The project, in fact, is imperious, and is as little likely to be successful as the attempts by scientific men to force Nature to reveal her secrets by "anticipation," or by dogmatic reason. God's spiritual kingdom, like his natural, *non imperatur nisi parendo.* The project is not prescribed by God, nor is it one to which we can reasonably expect him to conform.

Every intelligent defender of prayer has allowed a becoming sovereignty to God in answering the petitions presented to him. A number of persons are in the ward of a hospital; and there are Christian visitors praying for them, for their spiritual improvement and for their recovery — *if it be agreeable to the will of God.* In answering this prayer, God may provide that some, or many, or all, or that few or none, be cured, as it may be for the good of the persons praying, or the persons prayed for, or of the families and community to which they belong. And this sovereignty of God, always regulated by wisdom, is not to be interfered with by a proposal dated from the "Athenæum Club, Pall Mall," even if it has the sanction of one, who, conforming to the methods of science, has performed very effective experiments on heat and sound. Every one sees that the world might be thrown into inextricable confusion, were God necessitated to attend to such schemes, sanctioned in no way in his Word, or by the religion of Nature. In answering prayer, God has (to speak after the manner of men) to weigh a thousand circumstances, including the character of the men who pray, and the spirit in which they pray, and the character of those who are prayed for, and the influence they may exercise on society at large. A few years ago the late Prince Albert was in a raging fever; and hundreds of thousands were praying for his recovery. Must God answer these prayers by restoring the prince to health, and this whatever be the consequences? It is said, — on what I believe to be good authority, — that, shortly after the death of the prince, the wise and good Queen of Great Britain declined following the counsel of her advisers, when they wished to proclaim war against America, and she did so because her departed husband was always opposed to such a fratricidal proceeding. We may put the supposition that the prince, if alive, might not have had influence enough to stop the war; and that it could have been arrested only by the firmness of a woman inspired by regard for the dead. I enter in no way into the secret designs of God; but, putting the supposition, I ask whether even the hundreds of thousands praying would have been entitled to insist that the prince should be restored, when the result would have been the most unjustifiable and disastrous war of which our world has been the theatre? And might there not be equally weighty reasons why God should not spare more persons in the side of the hospital prayed for in the scientific experiment than in the other side not so cared for by man?

It is said of our Lord, that, at a certain place, he could not do many mighty works, "because of their unbelief." In order to his hearing prayer, in order to his answering prayer,

God requires faith, as large, at least, as a mustard-seed. With the evidence which every man has furnished to him of the existence, the love, and care of God, this requirement is most reasonable. It can be shown that there is admirable wisdom in God's plan of connecting the acceptance of prayer and the answer to prayer with a previous or contemporaneous faith. And it can be shown that our Lord showed equal wisdom in declining to work miracles on every occasion. He always refused to work them for mere empty display, or to gratify the wonder-seeking spirit of the Jews. Where they demanded signs in an arbitrary manner, he told them they had enough of evidence, and declared, that, if they believed not Moses and the prophets, neither would they believe, though one rose from the dead, — a declaration which was realized, when, a short time after, he rose from the dead, and the Jews continued as incredulous as ever. Suppose the proposed experiment succeeded for once, the scientific men would have some way of accounting for it, and would insist on the experiment being repeated once and again; which could be done only at the expense of deranging the whole of the delicately hung scales of Providence.

(2.) The project is not consistent with the spirit in which Christians pray. They pray because commanded to pray; they pray because it is the prompting of their hearts, commended by conscience; they pray because they expect God to listen to the offering-up of their desires; they pray because they expect God to grant what they pray for, so far as it may be agreeable to his will and their own good. But they shrink from praying as an experiment. A dutiful child would shrink from such an experimenting on the love of an earthly father. Such prayer, they feel, would imply doubt on their part, and might give offence to One who expects us to come to him as children unto a father. They fear that it might look as if they required him to answer prayer in a particular way, whether it may be for good or evil, and unjustifiably expose him to reproach, provided he refused to comply with the uncalled-for demand.

Christians would shrink from the idea of praying for the sick on the one side of a hospital, and not praying for those on the other. To reduce the whole project to an absurdity, we can conceive one body of men praying for one part of the ward, and another for the other part, and thus no choice left to God. True, there must be something like this when there is war between two countries; as, for instance, in the late war between France and Germany. But, in all such cases, God is judge, and may, we suppose, answer the prayers of the right side: nay, he may answer the prayers of both sides, giving the victory to Germany, and the trial to France, as a means of chastening her, and as she profits by it, and continues to pray, raising her to greater eminence in years to come.

(3.) These considerations show the negative side; but I cannot close without opening the positive side. What, then, induces a reasonable man to pray? What reason has he for thinking that his prayers will be answered? He has abundant reasons, quite as convincing as the scientific man has for believing, that, if he proceeds on the method of induction, he will make Nature reveal her secrets. But the evidence is not precisely the same in the two cases.

Every logician knows that there are various sorts of evidence, each convincing in its own department. There is one kind in physical science, of which Prof. Tyndall is master, but another kind in mathematics, and yet a third kind in morals and in practical duty. A father, let me suppose, recommends his son to follow virtue, to be temperate, chaste, honest, and benevolent, and assures him that he will thereby enjoy a much larger amount of happiness. But young hopeful professes not to be satisfied, and wishes to have clearer notions on the specific point, — whether a youth, indulging all his desires, with only a little prudence, may not have as much enjoyment as one who restrains them? And he insists that an experiment be tried with the boys of a poor-house, one half of whom are allowed every indulgence, while the other half are exposed to restraint. The wise father would at once cut off all such discussion, by showing that virtue is a thing binding on us, that, by its very nature, it is fitted to lead to happiness, and by pointing to the issues of virtue and vice seen in common life.

We are entitled to treat in the same way the proposal made to us in "The Suggestive Letter" forwarded to the "Contemporary Review." We show that prayer is the becoming expression of gratitude, the required confession of sins committed. We show that God commands us to pray: "Men ought always to pray." It is a confessed duty of revealed religion: it is, also, a duty of natural religion: it is the natural and proper outburst of a heart under the influence of becoming feeling. We believe that He who thus commands us to pray, will, in his own time and way, send an answer.

We should always be prepared to leave a sovereignty with God as to the means he may employ in answering prayer. I do not believe that God usually answers prayer by violating, or even changing, his own laws, — I mean physical laws. In answering prayer, God will have a respect to his own laws, ordered so wisely and so kindly. A violent, capricious interference with them, even in answer to prayer, might work irremediable mischief. But surely God is not precluded from answering prayer, because he hath instituted a wise economy in his physical government. I believe that God commonly answers prayer by natural means, appointed for this purpose from the very beginning, when he gave to mind and matter their laws, and arranged the objects with these laws for the accomplishment of his wise and beneficent ends, — for the encouragement of virtue, and the discouragement of vice, and, among others, to provide an answer to the acceptable petitions of his people. God, in answer to prayer, may restore the patient by an original strength of constitution, or by the well-timed application of a remedy.

The two, the prayer and its answer, were in the very counsel of God; and, if there had not been the one, there would not have been the other. The believer is in need of a blessing, and he asks it; and he finds that the God who created the need, and prompted the prayer, has provided the means of granting what he needs. But what reason can we have for believing that this experiment, devised in the Athenæum Club, Pall Mall, has a like place in the counsels of heaven?

He prays for things agreeable to God's will. He will not pray for any thing which God shows to be absolutely denied him. When his son is evidently dead, he will not pray that God would restore him to life in this world. As he prays for the sufferers on one side of a hospital, he will not be precluded from praying with equal fervency for those on the other side.

Led by such reasons to pray, he finds that his prayers are answered. His experience confirms his faith. Beginning the exercise in faith, he gains, as he continues, as abundant evidence of the power of prayer as of the power of any physical agent. In the course of years, and as he looks back upon his life, he can discover case upon case in which, unobserved by the world, his petitions have been granted; or, rather, he perceives, that, as he prays in duty and in faith, his whole life is ordered by the Lord. It is especially so, when his requests are for progress in spiritual excellence. When his prayers are hindered, he sees that his moral progress is hindered. When his aspirations are fervent, he finds that his soul is filled with peace, with comfort.

The proposal made in the letter forwarded by Prof. Tyndall is evidently regarded as likely to be troublesome to religious men. If they accept, it is expected that the issue of the experiment will cover them with confusion. If they decline, they will be charged with refusing to submit to a scientific test. It may turn out, however, that all that the letter proves is an utter ignorance, on the part of certain scientific men, of the kind of evidence by which moral and religious truths are sustained. I believe that the time has come when the intelligent public must intimate pretty decisively that those who have excelled in physical experiments are not, *therefore*, fitted to discuss philosophical or religious questions. Persons who do not follow the appropriate method in physical science will not be rewarded by discoveries. Those who decline coming to God, believing that "he is, and that he is a rewarder of them that diligently seek him," need not expect the blessings of religion. Prof. Tyndall has faith in the ordinances of nature; and he, and those who read his works, have profited by it. I have no evidence that he has studied so carefully the method of earning fruit in the kingdom of grace as in the kingdom of nature. But of this I am sure, that with a like faith in God, in his providence and word, as he has in science, he will reap a yet greater and more enduring reward.

James M'Cosh.

Princeton, N.J., U.S., Aug. 5, 1872.

VI.

CAPTAIN GALTON ON THE EFFICACY OF PRAYER.

THE SPECTATOR.

In No. 1,230, Aug. 3, 1872, pp. 974, 975, an editorial appeared under this title, which is now placed first.

Second includes letters, — by Astley Cooper in favor of the efficacy of prayer, by Protagoras against, and by J. J. Murphy in favor. These came out in the following number of "The Spectator," Aug. 10, pp. 1011–1013.

VI.

CAPTAIN GALTON CRITICISED.

THE scientific men, the men, that is, who hold it weakness to believe strongly any thing not supported by material evidence, — evidence which can be tested by the senses, — appear disposed to fight out their lifelong contest with the supernaturalists upon the battle-ground of the efficacy of prayer. In so doing, they are exhibiting considerable powers of strategy. With the instinct of heretics, — that is, of men who are resisting a widely received opinion, fighting an army more numerous than their own, — they perceive that this is the key to the position; that, if this ground is lost, all is lost; and perceive, also, that it is, of all the threatened points, the one most difficult to defend. We may say broadly, — what they see clearly enough, though they will not openly say it (a reticence which is not quite creditable to their fairness), — that if prayer is not answered, and cannot be answered, then there is in the Christian, or, rather, the religious, sense of the word, no God. If he exists at all as a sentient being, of whom man can form some limited and inadequate conception, he must have some relation to the sentient beings he has created, or has suffered to be created (for we will not exclude even the demiurgus theory); and he must have some free-will, as his creatures have; and if there is the relation, and if there is the free-will, there must be, to some extent, however limited, or however described, a power in him of answering prayer. He must be able to do something, if it be only what a man could do. How anybody can get out of that proposition, we confess ourselves wholly unable to conceive. It must be true under any conditions whatever, compatible with his existence at all. Suppose him even a limited Being, a Demiurgus, or that mere ultimate result of natural evolution of which some Atheists have dreamed (and that is the lowest view of the Godhead of which we can conceive); and still he must have some power, and some relation to men, and, with the power and the relation, some readiness, or, to speak more frankly, some moral obligation, to attend to prayer. Inability to do that is equivalent, for the purposes of man, to non-existence, to the absence of any relation between creature and Creator, which it is worth the trouble of analyzing or thinking about. With the idea of prayer, disappears the idea of God, and, with both, the whole of that body of supernaturalism which the physicists so bitterly hate. If prayer is a delusion, so are the creeds, churches are organized superfluities, priesthoods are impostures, revelations are only methods of securing a false importance for messages addressed by man to himself, — messages which may be more or less new or important in the field of morals, but are no more to be reverenced than similar messages in the field of science. In fact, every thing that physicists dislike disappears with belief in the efficacy of prayer, and the field is left clear for their faith (which we freely concede to them is, if not the only alternative, by far the most reasonable alternative), — the dominance of unalterable law, the perpetual evolution of physical effect from physical cause. At the same time, no position, as the physicists are well aware, is so difficult to maintain, by evidence which they will accept, as that of the efficacy of prayer. The very best evidence, namely, the experience of innumerable trustworthy persons, who in all ages have asserted that their prayers have been answered, they will not accept, indeed are precluded by their system from accepting; and of visible tests such as they would accept, there can be none, such test involving, *ex necessitate*, the coercion of a Being whom it is the first doctrine of those who believe in prayer to declare beyond the possibility of such coercion. Prof. Tyndall's challenge to pray for the inmates of one ward in a hospital, and not for another, and see what followed, is inherently absurd, not only for the reasons we gave the other day, but also for this, that, unless God possesses free-will, prayer is a waste of emotional energy; and, if he possesses free-will, he cannot be coerced into action in the manner the professor suggests he should be. We might as well test the royalty of an absolute monarch by demanding, that, if royal, he should grant the next petition addressed to him, even though granting it denied the freedom of his royalty. All that can be proved of prayer is, that its efficacy in some form is a necessary consequence of the existence of a God (for with Mr. Mill, we cannot admit the notion of God creating, and abandoning responsibility to the created); that the best men in all ages have not only believed it, but acted on the belief, without being ever deterred by the mass of experience to the contrary which they must have gradually acquired; and that keen, shrewd, nay, strange to say, sceptical intellects of the present day, in every country and under every condition, assert that their prayers have been answered. What other evidence is there, or can there be, for an assertion which most physicists credit, but which many would declare to be quite incredible, that the will — mere volition, without change of circumstances — can subdue or even banish existing pain? If the testimony of consciousness is valueless about the one thing, why not about the other?

While, however, we admit at once the enormous importance of the question, and the enormous difficulty of demonstrating our side of it to men who will not accept our data, we are not bound to submit patiently to arguments such as those by which Capt. Francis Galton, in this month's "Fortnightly," evidently thinks he has disposed of the efficacy of prayer. They are a little too trying to one's intellectual patience. Prof. Tyndall, though he scoffed with a kind of pride which seems to us out of place in a discussion in which he himself thinks certainty so difficult of attainment, did propose a test, which, though in our judgment so inapplicable as to raise doubts of his seriousness, was, at all events in form, the test which physicists would apply when experimenting with a view to certainty on any doubtful point of physical research, say, the efficacy of a new drug, or system of hygienic treatment. But Capt. Galton says no test is needed. The experience of mankind is already conclusive. Prayer never is answered, because doctors never have relied on prayers for the sick; because Christian sovereigns, who are universally prayed for, die, on the average, sooner than other rich people (probably from a family tendency, the Christian sovereigns of Europe being all members of a single family or clan, all, in fact, in one way or other, the descendants of one man); because missionary ships, which are prayed for, are no safer than slavers, which are not; because prayerful persons do not outstrip secular persons in the race of life, half our dukes, for example, being the descendants of kings' mistresses; because insurance-offices make no difference in favor of the pious; and because the clerics who pray for the success of their enterprises more than other people are not more successful in those enterprises. On this evidence, which we shall not dispute, Capt. Galton affirms that prayer has no efficacy; that belief in it will die, like any other superstition; and that it is, in all probability, a mere bleat, an expression of suffering, which, like the bleat of a sheep in pain, gives relief, we know not why.

We will not answer this astounding argument, as we might at first sight feel inclined to do, by declaring it physicism gone wild, a direct attempt to weigh mental consequences in a pair of brass scales, or by pointing out, that, according to the Christian belief which Capt. Galton is attacking, God has expressly declared that he does not limit his benevolence by men's deserving, raining equally on the just and unjust, or by asking Capt. Galton for proof that his pious persons ever pray earnestly without the earnest addition of a prayer that God's will shall be done, and not theirs; but will meet him face to face on his own ground, with his own method, and with a blank denial. In two cases, so large and so visible as to be better than any of his own, persons, about whom the presumption alike of prayer and of a prayerful spirit is greater than it is about any of those he names, have been enormously, almost miraculously successful. If it can be asserted of any human beings that they prayed for the diffusion of their ideas of faith, it can be asserted about the early Christians. If it can be asserted about any prayer, that it involved an antecedent improbability of realization, it can be asserted about that particular prayer. And in spite of all circumstances, of the reluctance of mankind, of the horror-struck resistance of princes, of the antagonism between those ideas and the instincts of mankind, of the weakness (as Capt. Galton would say) of those ideas, that prayer was heard, those ideas were diffused: that faith is the faith of the peoples who control the world. It is not we who are pressing that kind of evidence for prayer: we are simply accepting Capt. Galton's method, and giving him an overwhelming instance of a cause which was hopeless, which was prayed for, and which did win. The other instance is an even stronger one, on Capt. Galton's system of proof. He says that God is incessantly asked to grant sovereigns long life, and they die quicker than other people. We say, in return, that God is perpetually asked, in the same formal way, to protect the Papacy, and that in spite of all circumstances, of all oppositions, of, as we think, its own inherent and necessary tendency to death, — its pretensions being baseless, — the Papacy endures through the ages, and seems, as Macaulay said, as if it might survive all existing institutions. We do not say *post hoc, ergo propter hoc*, in the second instance we could not say it; but Capt. Galton, by the law of his method, is bound to say it for us. If the absence of protection for churches from lightning, and of kings from early death, are proofs that prayer is useless, then the victory of Christianity and the durability of the Popedom are greater, because more certain and visible, proofs that prayer is useful.

THE EFFICACY OF PRAYER.

[TO THE EDITOR OF "THE SPECTATOR."]

SIR, — The thanks of one so obscure as myself can be of very little importance to you for your recent able and interesting article in the controversy touching the efficacy of prayer; but they are due, not merely from me, but from hundreds of others; and you must allow me, as I am sure you will, judging from your well-known courtesy to correspondents, to tender them in my own name, and in the names of many of your readers with whom I have conversed on the subject. Your arguments are complete and strongly compact, so far as they go, and I can hardly hope to strengthen them; but concurrent lines of thought are like parallel streams when they meet, and swell the volume, and increase the force. On this principle, I would submit for consideration the following suggestions, which, I think, are not foreign to the point: —

1. The opponents to the belief in the efficacy of prayer assume that there is a promise that all prayers shall be answered. From whence do they get this assumption? Possibly they would answer, From the words which we regard as divine, "Ask, and ye shall have," &c. But surely such a promise as this must be fenced and limited. This may be illustrated by the relation of parent and child. We encourage our children to give us their confidence, and to make known to us their wants. But a want made known is not necessarily a want supplied, though it may be quite in our power to grant it; and this, because, in our superior intelligence and further-seeing wisdom, we know that the petition granted would bring with it mischievous or useless consequences. We withhold, not because we are unable to grant: we refuse the petition, not in indifference, but with the truest interest. The *child* sees not that now; but in after-life,

when the *man* comes to reflect, he understands and appreciates. May not all this apply to the divine Fatherhood of God? By the side of his intelligence and age, the most cultured, the most experienced, and the most advanced in age, are but the veriest children. And even more: some of us, as we look back, can see that the withholding the coveted gift by the divine Hand was the truest kindness, and the best answer to our prayer; and as we advance another stage, by a reasoning which we have a perfect right to use, we may expect, that "what we know not now, we shall hereafter."

2. And, if the words of the Master must be limited in the matter of the promise of the fulfilment of solicitations from the divine Hand, his life teaches exactly the same lesson. We who accept the teaching of the New Testament always speak of its Author's life as one of constant communion with the Father; but he asked for that which, at times, was denied him, though he said, "I know that thou hearest me always." Two memorable instances stand out. The Garden of Gethsemane was the scene of the one, and the hour that of the intense mental agony. Thrice was the prayer repeated, "Father, if thou be willing, remove this cup from me;" but it was not removed: it was drained to its last deadly drop. But in another way it was answered, "And there appeared an angel from heaven, strengthening him." The other was the case of St. Peter: "Behold, Satan hath desired to have you, that he may sift you as wheat; but I have

prayed for thee that thy faith *fail* not." But his faith did fail; and then came the oath, the cowardice, and the lie. Directly the Master's prayer was unanswered; *indirectly*, in another way, it was answered, — in the repentant, experienced, and more powerful man. I do not waste space in applying: the application is too obvious.

3. You rightly quote instances, and give historical facts, in illustration of your arguments for the truth and reality of prayer, — that belief which is so dear to tens of thousands. You might have gone to biography, if you had chosen. Allow me to give you an illustration. It was my happiness to know, near the scene of his labors, John Coleridge Patteson, whose apparently untimely death we are all lamenting. His was not a feeble intellect, or a superstitious nature, or a conventional, phrase-making tongue. He was a man of excellent parts in every way, and a believer in and a practiser of prayer. Above all things, he asked those who were interested in his mission to pray for its success; and his own life was fortified by it. The following incident in his life will illustrate what I mean: Some years ago he landed on an island, for the second time, which he was seeking to Christianize and civilize. He desired, after landing, to reach the chief's hut; and, to this end, he asked some natives, whom he saw on the beach, to guide him thereto. They consented; but, as he followed their leading, the idea came upon him that they meant treachery, as indicated by their vehement speech, gesticulations, and angry backward glances. Un-

easiness took possession of the bishop; and he feared for his life. Presently he came to an abandoned hut; and for a few minutes he left his guides, and those moments he employed on his knees in prayer. The effect, he used to relate, of thus commending himself to his divine Father, soul and body, was wonderful. All fear left him, and he came out of that hut regardless of consequences. And upon his treacherous guides the effect was no less wonderful. They gradually ceased to plot; and at last one of them turned, confessed the treachery, and offered to lead him back to his boat in safety. Was this the superstitious feelings of a weak mind, or the deep realities of the supernatural in answer to prayer?

I am, sir, &c.,

ASTLEY COOPER.

[TO THE EDITOR OF "THE SPECTATOR."]

SIR,—The article which appeared in your last issue on "Capt. Galton on the Efficacy of Prayer," though written with the general spirit of fairness characteristic of your journal, yet missed some points, and those very important ones, relating to the motives which actuate physicists in their antagonism to the doctrine of prayer as popularly held. One very important point, namely, the moral motive for their antagonism, seemed completely left out of sight. This moral motive, if we may be allowed so to term it, is the feeling which men have, who, being in full possession of knowledge, experience opposition to its application. This occurs most emphatically when any attempt is made to apply a scientific result to human life. To come down from generalities to concrete facts, it is impossible scientific men, however they may be imbued with the realities of science, can, in consequence, have intentions of making the idea of a God impossible, or even of upsetting all belief in what is termed the supernatural: what is really the case is, that they wish, in the interests of science and the conditions of human welfare, to get men to a rational comprehension of the results of science, so as to be able to apply them in a thoroughly complete way to human life, — ends impossible, so long as superstitions infect human practice, though perhaps unconsciously, in the ordinary ways of living.

The doctrine of prayer as popularly held is one which is completely in opposition to all positive science, professing, as it does, to be based on facts, which, if true, throw doubt on all inductive inference, throwing doubt, as it does, on all constancy in natural phenomena. It is very certainly to be inferred, from the facts exhibited by physiology and pathology, that the duration of life is dependent on the power any organism has for assimilating the elements necessary for keeping up the store of force in it requisite for performing its functions; upon the power it has of rejecting elements which are noxious or superfluous; and the power it has of resistance to changes in its surroundings hostile to it: yet the doctrine of prayer, if true, implies that these powers may be increased, if suitable appeal be made to the Deity. Now, belief in such doctrine, if worthy of the name of belief, must act most powerfully on men's practice, especially in matters of ordinary life. And though the belief in the doctrine of prayer is not very implicitly held by the generality of people now, yet it has implicit acceptance, and we find, as a result, general apathy in the cause of hygienic reform; and the path of the sanitary reformer is blocked by a dead-weight of stupidity, having its *raison d'être* in a vague notion that disease is a consequence of any thing at all, rather than inattention or direct violation of the physical conditions of health, and may be obviated, or even annihilated, by due ceremonial observances towards the Deity. And medical men find themselves checkmated in their efforts towards the cure and prevention of disease by superstitions more worthy of Central Africa than of Great Britain in the nineteenth century.

If God is a being any thing like one which we could term intelligent, and capable, likewise, of volition, we must, as the writer of your article says, believe him capable of answering prayer. But this is not the question in dispute, but, rather, "Has he made the universe in such a way as to *necessitate* his occasional *extra*-interference in ways at variance (for, whatever sophisms may be used to prove the contrary, the doctrine of prayer presupposes the idea of miracle; and the idea of miracle is that of contrary action to some law or laws of nature) with the order he has ordained phenomena should occur to us?" Now, in no province of knowledge is there more uncertainty than in that of medicine; and, therefore, in no other is there so much room for contradictory hypotheses: but from the analogies of demonstratively ever-present law in other regions of Nature, have we any reason to conclude medicine to be an exception to the dominion of law? Yet the doctrine of prayer amounts simply to the assumption that it is. Prayer has been, and is, asserted to be able to set up conditions different from what would have been, if prayer had not been used; and most particularly is this asserted in matters with which medical science has to do. If this assertion is true, it is very easy, as Dr. Tyndall has shown, to bring it to test. To term such an experiment as your writer does an attempt at coercing Deity seems absurd: it would simply be an appeal from humanity suffering in body and soul for want of his supporting presence; and what grander manifestation of himself could there be than in the healing of misery in this nineteenth century, as he is said to have done in the first? It is impossible that the relief of a suffering creature can be derogatory to the freedom of an infinitely benevolent Being. Mr. Galton's method of testing the efficacy of prayer is not so intrinsically absurd as your writer will have it to be, however matter-of-fact it may seem. For if, as is asserted, "the best men in all ages have not only believed, but acted on the belief, &c., and affirm that their prayers have been answered;" and if, at the same time, the doctrine of the efficacy of prayer is true, — it follows, that, even if the truth of that doctrine cannot be judged of from an individual and special case, we must, by all laws of probability, be able to discover evidences of its truth by comparison of the averages (and these are of health, long life, and success) in classes where it has undoubtedly been acted upon, and where we have every reason to presume it has not. But, from Mr. Galton's tables and statistics, it is very evident that the very opposite is the fact to what the truth of the doctrine would lead us to expect.

To quote the spread and power of Christianity, and the perdurability of the Papacy, as reasons for an opposite conclusion to Mr. Galton on his own line of argument, seems useless. For it is questionable whether, even in want of prayer, Christianity would not have spread as rapidly and extensively as it has done, judging from its history. And, with regard to the Papacy, any argument drawn from its continued existence is simply suicidal; for, in the first place, the popes have not been very notoriously long-lived after attaining the throne, especially the more enlightened ones, in spite of prayers for their well-being and long life in this world. And, secondly, if the Papacy, as a system, is proof of the efficacy of prayer, — a system of venerable imposture and self-delusion, according to the verdict of at least one-third Christendom, — it follows that the efficacy of prayer has no relation to the intrinsic merits or requirements of those who pray: therefore it will be better to trust to the providences given us in the knowledge of natural laws than to the capricious interference which has cursed and may curse humanity.

Though something might be said on the relations of the idea of prayer to that of natural law, it does not enter into the purpose of this letter; but the conclusions to be come to are, that the ordinary belief in the efficacy of prayer is based on no better grounds than any other superstition which has had similar generality of acceptance, say, for instance, the belief in judicial astrology; and that, the sooner the popular mind can be disabused of it, the better, if any progress is to be made towards a permanently elevated condition of civilized life, by the means given us in the results of physical and biological science.

I am, sir, &c.

PROTAGORAS.

[We recommend this letter to the consideration of those who think that only philosophers are discussing these questions, which had better, therefore, be kept out of newspapers. It is written by a bookseller's assistant in a provincial town. — ED. "SPECTATOR."]

[TO THE EDITOR OF "THE SPECTATOR."]

SIR, — In your notice of the 3d inst. of Mr. Galton's argument for the uselessness of prayer, you quote from him, without appearing to contradict it, that missionary ships, which are prayed for, are no safer than slavers, which are not. Is this certain? Many years ago, I heard it stated in a public lecture by James Montgomery, the poet (not to be confounded with Robert, or Satan Montgomery), that the annual ship to the Moravian missionary stations among the Esquimaux had never been lost in a period of about a hundred years, and was insured at half the usual rate for ships voyaging in the same seas, though I presume that Lloyds is as devoid of religious sympathies as the Stock Exchange. I think this fact worth noting, though my belief that God hears and answers prayer does not rest on this kind of evidence. I am, sir, &c.,

JOSEPH JOHN MURPHY.

OLD FORGE, DUNMURRY, CO. ANTRIM, Aug. 5, 1872.

[TO THE EDITOR OF "THE SPECTATOR.]

SIR, — Your reviewer, last week, repeatedly gives me a title of his own invention by styling me "Captain." I have never been in the army or navy in my life.

I am, sir, &c.,

FRANCIS GALTON.

42 RUTLAND GATE, Aug. 4, 1872.

[We had momentarily, but stupidly, confused Mr. Galton's history with that of a relative who was in the engineers. — ED. "SPECTATOR."]

VII.

THE EFFICACY OF PRAYER.

THE SPECTATOR.

FIRST, are presented letters which appeared in "The Spectator," No. 1,232, Aug. 17, by H., by C. W. Stubbs, by E., by E. D. W., and by Silvanus, pp, 1042–1044.

Second, the editorial of the same number, p. 1038.

Third, a letter from Francis Galton, which was published the following week, Aug. 24, p. 1073.

Fourth, letters from "The Spectator" of Aug. 31, by John Macnaught, by C. W. Stubbs, by A. Babington, by J. W. F., and by W. Y., pp. 1104–1106.

Fifth, a letter by M. G. G., p. 1139, and an editorial of Sept. 7, which summed up and closed the discussion on the part of "The Spectator."

VII.

THE EFFICACY OF PRAYER.

[TO THE EDITOR OF "THE SPECTATOR."]

SIR, — Because of the uniformity of Nature, and our confidence in the continuousness of the action of cause and effect (which is what our belief in uniformity amounts to), it does not surely follow that there is nothing in the whole universe that is not under the law of cause and effect. That is the conclusion to which natural science, in the hands of the physicists, to use that odious word, is more and more striving to drive us; and it is a conclusion which rests upon a very partial induction of the facts before us. This latest attempt, for example, to disprove the efficacy of prayer by an appeal to experience rests wholly on the assumption, that, if prayer have any validity, it, also, must be reducible under the category of cause and effect. That there may be anywhere in the universe a power outside of the causal chain able to modify the results of the action of the various links in that chain, without altering and varying the connection, so as to reduce all to arbitrariness, is a conception that seems utterly alien to the modern man of science. And yet what is the exercise of man's free-will but precisely a fact of that kind? If the universe be a storehouse of merely physical powers, which must, under certain unvarying relations, always produce the same precise connections and effects, — an evolution that goes on unalterably and unaltering, — obviously there is no room for man to modify by his action the results of these relations and connections. The writer of the article in last week's "Spectator," signed "Protagoras" puts the matter in a somewhat crude way, but still fairly and faithfully, as it is generally conceived by the physicist. There are, he says, certain assimilating forces in the human body; and the duration of the latter depends upon its assimilation of certain external elements, or consequent rejection of certain others. Now, if the doctrine of prayer be true, it must imply that these powers may be increased, if suitable appeal be made to the Deity. No more surely than the fact that man is able to introduce new directions in the connections of forces, that he can vary and alter indefinitely the relations in which they are to each other, and to independent objects, implies such a power. The whole history of scientific discovery is a record of the application, by man, of the laws and forces of Nature under such conditions as bring altogether new results; and yet there is no change in the character of the connection, and no addition of new elements other than those generated through the action of these forces themselves in their new conditions. All the elements that render a steam-engine possible were in the world before Watt's great discovery; and that discovery has not made any difference in the regularity and order of the causal connection of the forces employed. But a new result has been obtained simply by the new direction given to the action of these forces, by which man's power over Nature has been immeasurably increased, and he has been enabled to do what was before quite inconceivable. If such power over Nature rest with man, who is to modify so largely the action of natural laws and forces, by controlling them to the extent of giving to them new applications, why should it be deemed impossible for an infinitely higher intelligence, presumably the Author of these forces, to do the same? It is altogether fallacious to suppose that an answer to prayer, say, for restoration of health, can only be given by direct interposition, in the way of adding some new force or element to the chain of causes and effects by which physical existence is constituted. If man is capable of varying and modifying the action of these forces, so as to bring out new and different results by giving to them new directions, and if man is capable of receiving influence from God, why is it absurd to suppose that God may answer his prayers by suggesting, or leading to the suggestion to him, of the use of such means as will give the direction to the natural forces that must conduct to his restoration? In that case, the answer to prayer would give a fresh illustration of the reality of the connection of these forces, instead of being an arbitrary violation of it. The difficulty does not lie on the side of Nature or its order, then, but on the side of the relations between God and the human spirit. Yet once admit the existence of these two, and there is surely no inherent improbability in the assumption that such relations do exist, and that, therefore, man may ask, and God may answer. If a man may ask a fellow-man to do something for him, which implies the bringing-out of a result different from what the chain of cause and effect would do if left to itself, why may he not ask God to do so?

I am surprised that so acute a thinker as "Protagoras" seems to be should fancy there is any thing in his argument from the divine perfection against prayer. "Has he [i.e., God] made [he asks triumphantly] the universe in such a way as to necessitate his occasional *extra*-interference in ways at variance with the order [in which] he has ordained [that] phenomena should occur to us?" It is altogether an assumption that answers to prayer necessitate interference with any order. As we have seen, it is supposable prayer may be answered through and by means of the natural order, by simply using it in the way man does when he bends the order of phenomena to his own purposes. In regard to the supposed argument from the perfection of the divine plans, which should require no interference, why am I to assume that it is *not* part of these very plans that certain results should be brought about *by* prayer? If man has been gifted with such a constitution of mind and character, that prayer is needed to educate its highest capacities (and even Mr. Galton does not deny the possibly beneficial subjective influence of prayer), then the perfection of his Creator's plan implies that room has been left for such interferences in the way of guidance and direction as may be involved in answers to prayer. Nay, it is evident that it may very well be that only in and through these, as in and through the felt necessity to worship on the part of man, can the best results, both of physical and hyperphysical nature, be developed. Thus we are led to accept efficacious prayer as included in the divine scheme, without which that would not have been what it is; and therefore it is absurd to speak of it as an interference with it.

These objections and answers, however, only touch, as it were, the fringe of the great question. That remains, as hinted at the outset, — whether there is nothing in the whole universe but an invariable chain of cause-and-effect connections. Yet what we have already said disposes entirely of Mr. Galton's argument. On the hypothesis we have ventured upon, the interposition of the Deity to restore a patient o health cannot, from the nature of the act and its instruments, become a matter of observation. The causes that have acted upon the physical frame and constitution of the patient are matter of observation, and therefore, we say, his estoration is due to them; and the most quick-witted and harp-sighted of medical attendants could trace nothing but hem in the sphere of sense-perception. But, because that is so, it by no means, of necessity, follows that the influence of prayer is excluded. Who is able to affirm, in any case whatever, that certain suggestions leading to modifications of medical treatment, or certain minute mental and spiritual influences, — giving a special direction, it may be, to the patient's thoughts, and in the subtle association of mind and body, thereby giving opportunity for the *vis medicatrix* in the latter to operate, — are not due to Him without whose care no sparrow falls to the ground? We may give full scope to all the efforts of scientific men, and yet the region in which spiritual agencies and influences operate may not be affected or approximated to in the slightest measure; because, unless all our higher feelings and aspirations are a mockery and a lie, there is a region, above the sphere of cause-and-effect connection, in which free-will rules. Not that free-will implies the power of altering the constitution of Nature as a realm, or region, of cause-and-effect connections; for, though it is able to use Nature as its instrument, it can only do so by respecting its actual constitution. But free-will is not arbitrariness. If the higher philosophy of Germany have taught us any thing at all, it is that free-will and reason are identical; that law and liberty are reconciled as being one and the same principle, viewed from different sides. It is in the nature of reason to act rationally; and it would not be to act rationally to ignore the law or order, which is the rational element in the external world. The highest, the only true freedom, which is as far apart as possible from the arbitrariness of self-will, consists in such rational action; so that there can be no dread of the recognition of freedom leading to superstition. The reason within rejoices in recognizing the reason that is without. The latter, I say, is seen in the connection of cause and effect in Nature; for the constancy and universality of that relation can only be derived from reason, from thought. Hence the philosophers of mere experience have been driven to admit that cause and effect may not hold good as a universal law. It is Mr. Mill who has been guilty of the absurdity of averring the possibility that there may be regions in space where the law of cause and effect no longer holds good, and where two and two may *not* make four. Only from thought can we derive a law of universal necessity in things. But, because it is the law of reason that the relation is universally necessary in things, it does not follow that it is the same in what is the ruler, the master, the lord over things, viz., in thought itself, in the reason of an intelligent Being, which, as above all things, is capable of using and moulding these, and the order in them, for its purposes. But, if we once admit this,— and unless by reducing man to a machine, and depriving ourselves of all warrant for affirming even an order in the universe of matter itself, we must admit so much,—we can no longer deny that free intelligences, from a point outside of and above the chain of causes and effects in Nature, may modify the action by changing the directions of the causes and effects, and by introducing fresh combinations of them.

And if that be so; if man, as a free intelligence, can do so much, — surely we cannot refuse a like power to God, if we admit a God at all. Once this point is reached, there can be no room for a denial of the possibility of the efficacy of prayer through the influence of the Supreme Will upon inferior wills. The actuality of its efficacy is, of course, a further question; but the kind of evidence adduced by sceptical physicists in questioning, as well as the kind of evidence they require to prove it, are, I think I have shown, alike and altogether beside the question.

I am, sir, &c.,
H.

[TO THE EDITOR OF "THE SPECTATOR."]

Sir, — The question as between science and theology with regard to the efficacy of prayer is not, as you very justly pointed out last week, one which is engaging the attention of philosophers alone: it has a very near interest for men of all classes. It is all the more necessary, therefore, that we should keep ourselves quite clear as to what the exact point at issue is, and how much is involved in its retention or renunciation.

There are, as it appears to me, two entirely different views which may be held as to what is meant when we speak of God as granting a direct answer to our prayers. It is most important, I think, in this controversy that those two views should be kept perfectly distinct.

First, there is the view, held, I suppose, by a very large

majority of Christian people, that the man who is in the habit of praying to God with sincerity and faith has a right to expect that external circumstances will be ordered by the Deity in direct answer to his prayers.

Secondly, there is the view, held by an increasing number of thoughtful Christians, that, although God does undoubtedly grant a direct answer to the sincere prayer, yet that he does so, not by alteration of external circumstances, but by change in the suppliant's relation to circumstance.

In a word, both views imply the belief in direct answer to prayer; but, in the one case, it is regarded as being brought about by the alteration of circumstances with regard to the suppliant's position; in the other, by the alteration of the suppliant's position with regard to external circumstances.

Those who hold the first view naturally base their argument on the literal acceptation of such words as those in Matt. xxi., "All things whatsoever ye shall ask in prayer, believing, ye shall receive," and are honestly content to explain all failure in their petitions by assigning it to their own want of faith; while, on the other hand, those who uphold the second view, rejecting a literal interpretation of our Lord's words, citing his own prayer in the Garden of Gethsemane (which certainly, on the first hypothesis, must be regarded as a failure) in proof of their position, are content to insist on a rational interpretation of the letter, in accordance with the essential spirit of Christ's teaching.

Practically, of course, with the majority of Christian

people, neither of these views is held quite separately or accurately; but we are more generally suffered to modify one another according to circumstances. Such inaccuracy, of course, is natural enough; but, at the same time, it is, in all possibility, owing to the fact that such views are not kept quite independent one of another, that, in some instances (noticeably in the "Contemporary" letter), science has taken up a mistaken position. It is, of course, with the first view only, that science can claim any legitimate right to express an opinion. As one of your correspondents rightly said, "It is special prayer only, not all prayer, that is really obnoxious to the attacks of science." The assertion of actual change in external circumstances offers at once a definite field for experiment, and, therefore, for the operation of scientific reasoning. But with the second view, at present, at any rate, as it appears to me, science has simply no power whatever to deal. How far, and in what way, man's emotions may be influenced or controlled by man's *own* will, is surely a question which neither physics nor metaphysics have as yet at all satisfactorily explained, much less, therefore, how far, and in what way, they may be influenced or controlled by God's will. And this is, of course, what is involved in the acceptation of the second view.

But, on the other hand, with the first view, as I have said, science is entirely competent to deal; and, however much we may be inclined to object to the apparent spirit in which the question has been raised by the proposer of the experimental prayer-gauge, I think we must honestly allow, that not only is the attitude of science with regard to the efficacy of special prayer a reasonable one, but it is one that has actually, in this respect, influenced and modified theological opinion.

If it should happen, as a result of this controversy, that the second view of prayer should be finally accepted as the most truly in accordance with the spirit of Christianity, it will not be the first time that theology has gone to school to science to be taught the true meaning of its own books.

There is a possible result of this controversy which should not be lost sight of. To the Christian, the triumph of science on this question would probably be nothing but pure gain: to the churchman, it would necessarily raise occasions of some perplexity. In the Book of Common Prayer, there are not only prayers for special occasions, but prayers whose form presupposes that view, which, in expecting an answer, demands a distinct change in the course of natural phenomena. Yet to ask God to send even five minutes' rain, or to withhold it, science tells us, is to ask for the disarrangement of the whole order of the world, and, therefore, to demand a miracle. To any one, therefore, accepting the scientific conclusion with regard to what is called the law of the conservation of energy, a form of prayer which directly implies the creation of new force could not be conscientiously used. The only legitimate prayer to such a person would be one which took the form of a petition for a change, not of external circumstances, but of the relation of the suppliant to those circumstances. I do not see any intermediate position. But, if there be not, surely the clergy of the Church of England, at any rate, are in this dilemma: either they must accept that form of prayer which practically implies the continual working of miracles, or there must remain a considerable portion of that book which it is their duty to use in their public ministrations, to which they cannot give an unfeigned or honest assent. Surely a question is here raised, infinitely wider and more far-reaching than any that has resulted in the assertion that there must necesarily be a schism in the Church, if the reading of the Athansian Creed is to be left to the option of individual clergymen.

I am, sir, &c.,

CHARLES W. STUBBS.

GRANBOROUGH VICARAGE, BUCKS.

[TO THE EDITOR OF "THE SPECTATOR."]

SIR, — Your article on "The Efficacy of Prayer" has called forth so many letters, that I can hardly expect you to find room for mine. If any of your readers were capable of supposing that the subject is discussed "by philosophers only," they must be undeceived by this time. In fact, no question is more continually debated in conversation by persons of all shades of belief and all degrees of knowledge; and many must have been as grateful to you as myself for so good an opportunity of discussion, and especially for the tone of your own article.

I cannot but think that many (though not all) of the difficulties the question seems to involve are occasioned by a strange self-deceit. Do many persons really believe — not only think they ought to do so, but truly believe — that they can alter the intentions of the Most High by their entreaties? If so, how dare they ever open their lips to ask for any earthly boon whatever? How dare they ask for the life of their dearest friend, knowing, as they must, that God only can tell whether such a favor is not the most utter cruelty? Who that really had no doubt of the result would ask for worldly prosperity or success; nay, who would dare to pray for what he believed to be the most truly religious object? I cannot believe that any one would really incur so fearful a responsibility. All the efforts that we make towards an object will, as we trust, be mercifully frustrated, if God should see that their success is undesirable; but to expect him to change from his plans to ours, at our request, would truly be to believe, that, when we asked bread, he would give us a stone. As to the question of fact, it seems to me decided, as far as visible results go, by one circumstance. There is probably no purer or more fervent prayer offered on earth than the prayer of a mother that her son may grow up a good man: we can conceive no reason why it should fail; but the son does not always grow up good. God forbid that we should therefore suppose her prayer is in vain! but certainly it does not produce a visible answer, such as a large class of persons think they expect.

The truth I believe to be that many persons have no conception of prayer, except as a request for some specified favor. They think, truly, that God has promised to hear prayer: therefore they feel bound to believe that he will grant the favor. Surely this is not what prayer means. It is not the intercourse an earthly father desires with his children. He would have them speak to him of every thing, — their joys and sorrows, their faults and resolutions, no doubt, also, their fears and wishes; but he would not have them speak only when something was to be got, or suppose him to be inattentive to them, unless he gave them every thing they asked. So we should make our prayers rather communion than entreaty. We should tell our Father in heaven all that we feel, or fear, or wish. If it is important to us, we know he will not think it too trifling for him to hear; but to suppose that the getting or not getting a special boon is the test of his existence, or his love, is a great and unhappy mistake.

It may be said, that, on this view, we cannot have evidence from the result of our prayers. We cannot; nor is it to be expected that we should, — such evidence, at least, as can be convincing to another person. The theory of visible and immediate answers raises at least as many difficulties as it removes. But we who already believe shall find, that, the more true communion we have with God, the more he becomes an actual living Being to our feeling and conviction, not a mere force to be moved, or not moved, as the case may be, by another force.

I am, sir, &c.,

E.

[TO THE EDITOR OF "THE SPECTATOR."]

SIR, — If your correspondent "Protagoras" finds "the doctrine of prayer, as popularly held," actually interfering with sanitary reforms in his own town, he may be right to protest; but he should not assume that scientific investigations and exposure of "popular" notions of this or any other subject are the same thing. He should examine and test the language of the great thinkers — say, such men as Maurice and Bunsen — who have strictly and habitually asked themselves what they meant by prayer, and who did, as the result of such inquiry, continue to believe that it had a meaning, and was no mere popular superstition. He would then find that the question is one of premises; that its "scientific" solution depends entirely on the "scientific" solution of the previous questions, — What is God? what is the relation of man to God? Prayer may be the utterance of

"An infant crying in the night,
An infant crying for the light,
And with no language but a cry."

But whether that cry has a meaning, depends on whether, as a fact, that child "crying, knows his father near." Or if we contemplate God as a Creator and Sovereign, as well as a Father, prayer may still have a "scientific" reality, if we believe — as many learned and accurate thinkers have believed, after a life-long investigation of the subject — that the world has been created, and is actually governed, by a God. Such a belief no more necessarily involves a superstitious belief in miraculous interference with the laws of Nature than does the belief that the personal guidance and control which Mr. Brassey exercised over his agents, contractors, and workmen, was essential to the making of his railways, implies that every act of such contract of guidance was a miracle; or that there is a conceivable, an actual, guidance of the Government of England by Mr. Gladstone, which neither, on the one hand, leaves the State to work by itself without any interference, nor, on the other hand, interferes by miracle. Why is the personal guidance of the machinery of the universe by God less conceivable than the government of certain portions of it by men? And why should not God recognize conditions under which men may act with God in carrying on that government? Prayer has a scientific basis for those who believe in an actual relationship between God and man, however true it may be that many popular superstitions have been raised on that basis. And, if "Protagoras" will investigate the question scientifically, he must begin with that previous question which underlies it. There is no real argument between men who are not agreed on their principles.

I am, sir, &c., E. D. W.

[TO THE EDITOR OF "THE SPECTATOR."]

SIR, — I have read with much interest the letters in your paper upon the efficacy of prayer. I now venture to intrude the few following remarks upon that subject, as it appears to me that your correspondents have entirely overlooked, or not considered, the points to which I wish to draw attention.

The *apparent* answering of any prayer is no proof that it has received the special attention of the Almighty. I believe this will be rendered clear by the following observations: (1.) The existence of a God is considered admitted, and that his attributes are omnipotence, omnipresence, and omniscience, infinite love, and infinite perfection. (2.) As all things emanate from him, he being perfection itself, it follows that his works must be perfect. Putting aside all considerations of the morality of man praying to infinite Perfection to alter creation for his especial benefit and temporary necessity, is it possible for the Almighty to change what *is?* It must be borne in mind the attributes of God *prove* that alteration of his plans is impossible, because to presume the possibility of change is at once denying the infinite perfection of the Almighty. (3.) Can man, remembering always the attributes of God, deny, that, when a prayer has presumably been answered, the same results would not have followed, had the prayer never been uttered? If he is infinite perfection, he must have created all that is requisite for man; and to request him to provide other than that which exists implies a complete want of faith in his eternal providence. Of course, if these attributes should be denied, God is at once reduced to the position of a more or less powerful, and more or less beneficent Being, according to the ideal of any individual.

I am, sir, &c.,

J. SILVANUS.

THE EFFICACY OF PRAYER.

WE have before us a very curious proof of the interest taken by the educated and semi-educated class in the subject of the efficacy of prayer. It is a heap of letters, all about prayer, sent us for publication in two days, which would fill, as nearly as we can calculate, sixteen pages of this journal. One or two of them, we are bound to say, are mere sermons; but the majority are attempts, sometimes by half-educated men, at a frank and close reasoning-out of the matter. As "The Spectator," though deeply interested in theological questions, is not specially devoted to theology, and is desirous of treating it from the lay observer's point of view, we must refrain from publishing more than a selection from this mass, and can hardly hope that the excluded will approve, or understand, the principle upon which the selection has been made. The majority of the letters before us are written, as was natural, from the supernatural side; but a great many of them bear trace of a feeling we had scarcely expected to find, — a strong desire on the part of many persons who believe in a sentient God, and of some who are apparently Christians, to get rid of the difficulties of the subject by reducing, without denying, the efficacy of prayer. They seem to be aware of the direct connection between the question of the possibility of an answer to supplication, and the existence of a sentient Being ruling the universe, and want to retain prayer as a spiritual exercise, but to find for it another and sufficient spiritual use. Of course, they are in part successful. It is quite true, as one correspondent suggests, that the emotion of prayerfulness, or state of being prayerful, is, when sincere, beneficial; and true also — though not, we fear, absolutely true in all cases and with all men — that the habit of prayer, even when ineffectual, would tend to produce a habit of submissiveness to the divine Will, which might be the very highest attitude of the human soul. It is also true that the majority of believers have a belief as strong as an instinct, that, in praying, they are obeying the will of God, — "co-operating" with him, as one clergyman expresses it, — and therefore renewing their moral vigor; and truest of all, that, without prayer, there can be no sense of individual communion with God, the point which Canon Liddon, in his collection of lectures just published, seems disposed to press so strongly. But then it is also true, that if prayer is never answered, and never can be answered, and we know that it never is or can be, this becomes a tainted method of spiritual exercise, tainted with conscious unreality and sham. A prayer is more than a monologue in the vocative case; and to join in a long series of supplications, or to make supplication for one's self, while fully confident that no supplication will be heard or attended to, is a great deal too much like lying solemnly.

Moreover, it seems to us that most of these arguments are beside the point at issue, certainly beside that one raised in the publications with which the controversy commenced. The physicists are not trying to assert that prayer, or any other mental operation, may not be attended with benefit of some kind, — just as the lamb's prayer, the bleat, may, in some unknown way, tend to relieve its suffering, — but to show that to expect an answer is unreasonable to absurdity; is to expect that the continuity of cause and effect — which, as far as observation extends, is never broken, and, as they maintain, never can be broken — shall be violated for the sake of an individual. This is clearly the argument upon which the whole discussion turns, and the one which impresses itself even upon the orthodox; for it is this which, in all their solutions, they are endeavoring — of course quite unconsciously — to evade. We cannot see why they should evade it, or why — admitting fully and earnestly, as we have throughout tried to do, the magnitude of the intellectual difficulties which surround the whole subject — they should feel more difficulty in ascribing to God this power, than, say, the power of creation, or conversion, or any other of the actions which we habitually, and, as we think, on good evidence, ascribe to the divine Will. If he exists at all, — and we are just now addressing those who admit that cardinal proposition, — he must have some power; and the difficulty of comprehending or defining the limits of that power is not greater in one case than in another. Our Buckinghamshire correspondent, for example, seems to be greatly perplexed by the prayer for rain, and suggests, though he does not quite say, that this, at all events, must be ineffectual. Why? That it would usually be ineffectual may be granted at once; for it would be nine times out of ten one of those selfishly stupid prayers, which no Being at once good and wise could properly be expected to grant. For why, on any theory of his love, should he grant John's desire, when to grant it is to refuse Joseph's? But we could imagine a tenth time, a time of drought in a tropical land, when the heavens were as brass, and the earth as iron, and all hearts and brains absorbed in the desire of rain till the spiritual life was in danger of being overmastered as by a lunacy, when the selfish supplication might become a true and an unselfish, and even a spiritual prayer; and why should it not be answered then? To say it *might* not be is reasonable; for to say that God knows best whether it is better for his usual modes of action to be supplemented by a new one, or for the people of Orissa to perish, is not to ascribe to him any incredible degree of wisdom, — little more than the wisdom of a great general who lets a regiment perish that a people may be free; but to say that he *could* not answer it is, at all events, to deny him creative power, to go infinitely further than a very strong physicist, Dr. Carpenter, is, in his inaugural address to the British Association, prepared to go. He, unless we mistake him in a curious way, holds that the final end of physical research may be, and probably will be, the discovery that a mind was the final cause; and, if it can be the cause of matter, why not of the phenomena of matter? It may be terribly difficult for the mind to conceive of God creating a cloud, or modifying by volition the physical conditions of a sick man; but it is not *more* difficult than to conceive his creating any thing at all which did not exist before, or changing the operations of a man's mind by invisible agency, or issuing the law according to which, even on Dr. Carpenter's apparent theory, Nature maintains her immutability. That legislation surely is a high effort of absolutism. That is no answer to Dr. Tyndall, or the writer he edits, or to Mr. Galton; but it seems to us a complete answer to any one who accepts a sentient Creator, even though he thinks, in defiance of common justice, that a creator may create, yet be irresponsible to himself for the fate of the created. Why God should so exert his authority at the request of a man is a different matter, depending on the proof that the creative mind must establish, and does establish, relations with his creatures, which, in some way, must be sympathetic or beneficent; but that he *can* is included in the argument that he is Creator. The difficulty of miracle — that is, of the intervention of a power whose laws we have not ascertained — is but part of the difficulty of conceiving a creating Being at all. No conceivable miracle is equal to that implied in the words Longinus thought so sublime: "And God said, 'Let light be.' Light was." It is not more difficult to conceive that God blighted a fig-tree, man needing that particular lesson, than to conceive that he issued and maintains a law, under which all fig-trees, under certain conditions, must be blighted. Mr. Silvanus's retort, that the fig-tree could not be blighted except under the conditions, because departure from the conditions would imply their imperfection, which, they being God's work, is impossible, is either no retort at all, or is only a restatement of the old difficulty of free-will. If God cannot change aught of his eternal law, he is not free, is more bound than me. But why is it incredible that one of the eternal conditions of matter should be amenability to the volition, which, on Mr. Silvanus's theory, created it? A correspondent in another page has put this point, as we think unanswerably: "In regard to the supposed argument from the perfection of the divine plans, which should require no interference, why am I to assume that it is *not* part of these very plans that certain results should be brought about *by* prayer? If man has been gifted with such a constitution of mind and character, that prayer is needed to educate its highest capacities, — and even Mr. Galton does not deny the possibly beneficial subjective influence of prayer, — then the perfection of his Creator's plan implies that room has been left for such interferences, in the way of guidance and direction, as may be involved in answers to prayer. Nay, it is evident that it may very well be that only in and through these, as in and through the felt necessity to worship on the part of man, can the best results, both of physical and hyperphysical nature, be developed." At all events, it cannot be fair to accept the power of God to create, and deny his power to modify his creation. Nor, so far as we can see, is it fair to talk of the magnitude of any effort of the supreme volition. We do not know what is great or little to God; do not even know, that, in his creative work, there can be inequality of effort.

We are most anxious not to introduce any reference to Scripture, which, to most of our opponents, would seem beside the mark, and, to some, the taking of an unfair advantage; but it has interested us to notice that the "refusal" of Christ's prayer in Gethsemane has, in some minds, definitely decreased the idea of the efficacy of prayer. Mr. Stubbs mentions this; and accidentally another correspondent asks if it is not proof against the Orthodox view; and a third quotes it as proof positive that earnestness is no guaranty for acceptance. As Christ prayed only as a human being, as his prayer was that God's will might be done, and as his prayer in his agony was contrary to the perpetual interest of all mankind, the illustration seems a weak one; but we want to ask why it is so universally asserted that the prayer was rejected? The prayer was not to be relieved from death, but from the cup of bitterness; and it seems to us, accepting, of course, the literal accuracy of the record, that the narrative may mean that it was answered; that the certainty which overcomes that bitterness had arrived when he conveyed the assurance to the penitent thief, though it was again lost in physical agony; that in the words, "It is finished," was announced a new and full conception of the whole plan of his life, which must have extinguished forever all that was of bitterness in the cup. That is, perhaps, but a "view;" but it is at least sufficiently borne out to deprive an argument upon which too much stress is laid by many minds of its operative force.

THE EFFICACY OF PRAYER.

[TO THE EDITOR OF "THE SPECTATOR."]

SIR, — I thank you for having opened your columns to discussion upon the efficacy of prayer, and to have so well acted as moderator, in a matter which deeply touches the feelings of many men, as to have enabled the discussion to be carried on with mutual forbearance and respect on the part of the disputants.

My object in writing now is to endeavor to confine the discussion to what I conceive to be strategic points, though they are commonly neglected, and are usually but indirectly aimed at, by your numerous correspondents. Those who deny the right of appeal to statistical inquiries upon the efficacy of prayer assume implicitly two propositions, both of which I gainsay, and which I will now explicitly state. They assert, first, that the desire to pray is intuitive to man (let the word pass, for the moment) ; secondly that the cogency of intuition is greater than of observation. I maintain, on the other hand, that the desire to pray is not intuitive, and, even if it were, that the cogency of intuition is less than that of observation. As regards the meaning I assign in this letter to "intuitive perceptions," I am perfectly willing to accept the widest definition my adversaries can reasonably desire. I do not wish to haggle about narrowing the limit: it is in no way necessary to my argument that I should do so, therefore I will concede enormously, and will allow that all perceptions or feelings strongly developed in the average man may be reckoned as intuitive to the human race. Now, I assert that the desire for prayer is not one of these feelings, but that it is an artificial creation of theologians ; also that the class of similar feelings which *are* intuitive are such as obedience to dreams, incantations, and witchcraft, fear of the evil eye, belief in demoniacal possessions, exorcising, coercion of an angry spirit by some tom-tom ceremony, fetish-worship, and taboo. The savage does not pray by natural inclination ; but the missionary *teaches* him to pray ; and as, at the same time, he preaches to him on the existence of a God who listens to prayer, precept to pray is a logical sequence of that instruction. The savage believes in what the missionary tells him, because the missionary is avowedly a more instructed man than himself in many things, and he is certainly in earnest: therefore the missionary's deity is accepted by the savage, and the converted heathen is taught to pray.

In modern civilization, the action of the mother upon the belief and habit of the child resembles, in many respects, that of the missionary upon those of the savage. She tells him loving tales about God's watchful care, and of his answers to those who kneel and speak to him; and she joins his little hands together, and sets him on his knees, and *teaches* him, with caressing earnestness, to pray for temporal blessings, from the very dawn of his intelligence. What wonder that this nursery theology should pervade his life, and that it should be so associated with his deepest feelings that he should at last believe it to have been intuitive? His belief is confirmed by the events of his after-life; for, on all its solemn occasions, it is the habit for the clergyman to step in, and to consecrate them by prayer. He is present by the death-bed, by the marriage-altar, and by the baptismal font; he usually superintends early instruction; and he has by custom the opportunity and unrestrained right of preaching and praying before large congregations on every seventh day. Again I ask, What wonder is it that a habit of prayer, and a sense of its necessity, should be formed, which seem, until their sources have been analyzed, to be one of primeval origin?

My second point is easily disposed of; namely, that, even

if the belief in prayer were intuitive, its cogency ought to be considered inferior to that which is prompted by the observation of facts. My argument is this, — I do not care to go into the metaphysics of the matter, but would simply point out that the very theologians who insist on the supreme authority of religious intuition are precisely the men who have already most prominently denied it in practice. Their predecessors at the time of the Christian era, and for hundreds of years subsequently, nay, even men of the present time in Catholic countries, have believed in the divine origin of dreams and auguries, in ordeal and in duel, in lots after prayer, in blessing and in cursings, in witchcraft, in miraculous cures, in demoniacal possessions, and in exorcisms. All this the theologians of the present English Church have quietly suppressed as of "superstitious" origin. They also complacently ignore that their predecessors have been beaten along their whole line by statistical inquiries; for it is by more or less unconscious use of statistics that the belief in ordeal, duel, augury, and the rest, has disappeared; and, now that theologians are summoned on statistical grounds to surrender a belief which I have shown to have much less claim to be considered as intuitive, they start with *naïve* indignation, as at a previously unheard-of and most unreasonable interference. You will observe that the views advanced in this letter could be much more strongly enforced by an elaborate essay; but "sapienti verbum sat," and I write concisely, at the risk of weakening my case, in order to induce those who may answer me in your columns to be equally concise and pointed.

I am, sir, &c.,

FRANCIS GALTON.

THE EFFICACY OF PRAYER.

[TO THE EDITOR OF "THE SPECTATOR."]

SIR, — Mr. Galton's interesting letter in your paper of yesterday induces me to trouble you with a few observations in reply to that gentleman, and on the subject generally. With reference to your correspondent's first point, must it not be conceded, that, even though prayer be not intuitive, it may be effective of its proper purposes? Hardly any one would maintain that the multiplication-table or the 47th proposition of the first book of Euclid come to man intuitively; but yet they are very effective means for the accomplishing of certain ends. Similarly, prayer may be efficacious, even though it be, as Mr. Galton thinks, the result of instruction, and not of intuition.

If this be so, one need not, in this connection, examine your correspondent's other point, touching the comparative cogency of intuition and observation. But now, to come to the great question of the efficacy of prayer, and to the challenge to have a ward in some hospital set apart as a prayer-test.

So far as one prays to achieve some purpose one's self, it may probably be assumed, and will scarcely be questioned, that earnest desires, reverently stated before God as even a *supposed* friend, will be purified of some unattainable and unreasonable cravings; and the same process of stating desires to one's God will strengthen resolution, and will insure a wiser selection of means for attaining the wished-for end. To this extent, then, perhaps, it may be allowed that prayer is efficacious.

But then there is intercessory prayer. What of it? May we not say, that so far as it is employed in the manner sketched above, and so far as it sets the petitioners to work devising and executing the best methods for superinducing health and happiness and good morals for those on whose behalf supplications are made, to this extent prayer is efficacious? But limits to its effectiveness become more and more perceptible. With reference to good wishes before Heaven, for ourselves and for our neighbors, the poet's words are in no small measure true: —

> "And all your views may come to nought
> When every nerve is strained."

So, again, but more obviously still, when prayers are made for rain, or dry weather, or success in war, or any such matter, opposing entreaties are morally certain to be addressed to the Deity; and both sets of desires cannot be accomplished at the same time and place; so that, supposing, as we may, each petition to come from equally acceptable hearts, here is another source of limitations to the efficacy of prayer. Something might be urged to the effect that the praying farmer will be most provident in varying his crops, and doing the best that can be done to make hay while the sun shines. But those who doubt the efficacy of prayer would reply, that it is the wisdom, and not the piety, of the agriculturist, that secures his crop; or the sternness, and not the religion, of the Cromwellian, that wins the battle.

Besides, if we pass from prayer generally, to Christian prayer in particular, must not the widest hopes and precepts and promises of the New Testament be interpreted and limited by the fact that the Master himself, when he prayed, repeatedly and with intensest earnestness, for deliverance from a death of anguish and ignominy to himself accompanied by wretched sin in those around him, only prayed conditionally: "If it be possible;" "nevertheless, not my will, but thine be done"? Surely Christian prayer for whatsoever we wish in Christ's name, the "effectual, fervent prayer of a righteous man," can only be addressed to the heavenly Father with this same conditionality attached, by implication or expressly, to its every sigh, its every thought, its every word. But if this be the very nature of Christian prayer; if we can only ask recovery of health for ourselves or others, if such be the Father's will, — what becomes of the proposed test by a hospital ward? *Christian* prayer must be for *all* the wards and *all* their patients, that they may *all* recover, *if God will.* As likely as not, it may be in his wisdom that the ward not allotted to the necessarily non-Christian supplications shall have the larger proportion of recoveries. Look at it as we may, the test shows itself to be inapplicable.

And yet it may be held, not as a matter of miracle, in the popular conception of that term, but as a result of common observation, that in the case of two hospitals, one of which is conducted in careful but non-religious ways, and the other in careful and Christian ways, the patients in the latter would, generally, gain peace of mind and hope in such wise, that they would be more likely to recover health than the no less skilfully tended sufferers in the former.

To sum up, this letter is intended to maintain, that, whether the desire to pray be intuitional or acquired, prayer is, in a large measure, effective in attaining the direct objects prayed for; and, where this may not be, it soothes the mind, and strengthens the suppliant for enduring manfully that which is the inevitable behest of beneficence; and, yet further, this letter maintains, that, apart from Christian prayer necessarily involving such efforts for the objects prayed for as would be credited with the special cures in the ward-test contemplated (if that test were otherwise possible), it is simply and absolutely impossible, by reason of the conditionality which attaches as an essential characteristic to all Christian prayer.

I am, sir, &c.,

JOHN MACNAUGHT.

LONDON, Aug. 25, 1872.

[TO THE EDITOR OF "THE SPECTATOR."]

SIR,—I must confess to have experienced a certain amount of difficulty in apprehending the exact force of Mr. Galton's argument with regard to what he considers "strategic points" in the present discussion.

He asserts that those who deny the right of appeal to statistical inquiry upon the efficacy of prayer implicitly assume two propositions; viz., that the desire to pray is intuitive, and that the cogency of intuition is greater than observation. These two propositions he proceeds to disprove. Now, granting, for the moment, that he has succeeded in doing so, I do not clearly see how he considers that he has advanced his position with regard to the inefficacy of prayer. It appears to me that Mr. Galton's argument is entirely a work of supererogation.

I am not aware that those who profess belief in the efficacy of prayer are under the necessity of arguing that the reason of holding such a belief is a matter of intuition with them. The reasonable Christian, no more, I suppose, than the scientific man, is liable to maintain that a proposition which is not of the nature of an axiom is incapable of proof. Yet Mr. Galton's letter seems to be based on a contrary opinion. The process of his reasoning is very simple. He first makes the assumption that those who oppose his view consider intuition to be the only ground for prayer. He proceeds to prove that the *desire* to pray is not intuitive. This he considers equivalent to proving that the belief in the efficacy of prayer is absurd. Surely the demonstration is not quite complete.

The objection of those who deny the right of appeal to statistical inquiry in this matter is not that such a method is an appeal to experience, when it should be an appeal to intuition, but, rather, that it is an appeal to only one branch of experience, and that a branch which science is not competent to investigate. If Mr. Galton means to maintain that there is nothing which is not within the range of scientific inquiry, he should say so. The discussion would be much simpler. To assert that there is no efficacy in prayer, because there is no God to pray to, would be a plain enough statement. Perhaps this is a "strategic point" in reserve.

I am, sir, &c.,

CHARLES W. STUBBS.

GRANBOROUGH VICARAGE, BUCKS.

[TO THE EDITOR OF "THE SPECTATOR."]

SIR, — Can you allow me space for a few words on the subject of the "Efficacy of Prayer"?

1. It seems to me that Mr. Galton, and those who think like him, have, as against the Christian, avoided the main point at issue. Surely the Christian argues from the existence of a loving Father in heaven to the efficacy of prayer, and not from the efficacy of prayer to the existence of a personal God. It is because Christ has revealed to us a heavenly Father who loves us with a love of which we can only see a faint reflection in the highest earthly affection,

that we Christians are emboldened to offer up our petitions to him in trustful and childlike confidence. It would be to me the most glaring contradiction in terms, to believe in a Deity such as the God of the New Testament, and yet to hold, either that he does not heed my prayers, or else that he cannot answer them if he would. Let Mr. Galton prove to me that Christianity is an imposture or a delusion, and he will have no need to pelt me with statistics in proof of the inefficacy of prayer.

2. Mr. Galton says of his opponents, "They assert, first, that the desire to pray is intuitive to man." I assert nothing of the sort in the sense in which Mr. Galton understands the words. I hold that the desire to pray is "intuitive" just so far as the belief in a personal God is "intuitive," and no farther. And this belief in a personal God I shall certainly hold to be "intuitive" and "necessary," in the highest sense of the words, in spite of the undoubted fact that the vast majority of the human race have never held the belief at all.

3. "But," it is urged, "examine statistics; see with what difficulties your doctrine of prayer is beset!" Granted. But I assert, in reply, that the highest spiritual truths are precisely those which are and must be beset with the greatest difficulties. I hold, with Dr. Newman, that the fundamental spiritual truth, without which all religion can be little better than a mockery, the belief in a personal God, is the one point of faith which is encompassed with most difficulty.

Yet this being of a God is a truth which is borne in upon my mind with a conviction as irresistible as the conviction of my own existence. That this subject of the efficacy of prayer is in many respects painfully perplexing, I readily admit. But I venture to think that the Christian solution is at least as satisfactory as that of the philosopher, who, like the ancient sophist, insists upon making man the measure of all things, and metes out with the iron measuring-rod of statistics, and averages the influences of that Spirit which "bloweth where it listeth."

I am, sir, &c.,

A. BABINGTON.

MARLBOROUGH COLLEGE.

[TO THE EDITOR OF "THE SPECTATOR."]

SIR, — If the desire to pray is, as Mr. Galton asserts, "not intuitive" to humanity, but "is an artificial creation of theologians," what made the theologians pray? Out of nothing, nothing can come, is as true of mind as of matter. If a future missionary should ever find a tribe of savages who have no belief in invisible power, and no feeling of worship, he will find it a hard, if not a hopeless task, to create such a feeling. The records of Christian missions clearly prove that the missionary has not to create the inclination to pray, but merely to direct the existing worship of the unseen to a worthier object. Indeed, Mr. Galton, in admitting fetish worship among the "class of feelings which *are* intuitive," virtually concedes his first strategic point; for it is the instinct or intuition of worship, not its perfection, that the theologian claims to be common to humanity. If we believe in the existence of a personal Deity, the Father of all men, it is surely not too much to suppose that he condescends to every aspiration, however feeble and imperfect, of the lowest of his children. When men could find no better mode of judging than the result of a trial by ordeal or duel, I believe that God, even through such imperfect means, did often "defend the right." If he had invariably done so, the process of mental and spiritual growth would have been arrested. If it is true generally, as Mr. Galton believes, that the theologians of the present English Church do not believe in the divine origin of dreams, miraculous cures, demoniacal possessions, and exorcisms, so much the worse for that Church, since its leaders have ceased to believe in the faith of their Master.

Mr. Galton's second point is, to use his own expression, easily disposed of. Worship of the invisible is intuitive, if by intuition is meant that it exists, and has existed in every age and nation; and it has what Mr. Galton considers the superior cogency prompted by the observation of facts. Christians need have no fear of the result of statistical inquiries as to the efficacy of prayer, provided that the inquirers are men thoroughly qualified to deal with the subject. I am, sir, &c.,

J. W. F.

[TO THE EDITOR OF "THE SPECTATOR."]

Sir, — The continued interest manifested in this discussion is a very satisfactory indication of moral earnestness pervading a great number of liberal thinkers. Will you accept the following crude contribution to it, *quantam valeat?*

How are we to reconcile the reasonableness of prayer with the existence of a divine Being, who, from the first, planned every thing in perfect wisdom, and who, as we must suppose, from the first foresaw the whole infinite series of causes and effects that would be evolved from his creation? Can the divine purposes be changed? Can they become different in the result from what they were in the original intention? We can scarcely suppose it. How, then, can prayer under any circumstances be effectual? Perhaps some indication of the answer may be found in the following considerations.

We conceive all events to have their source in the will of the divine Mind, and that the "laws of nature" are merely the expression of that will. Although the divine Mind be endowed with perfect foreknowledge, we must still conceive it to be conscious of a *succession of* impressions, *i.e.*, of a past, a present, and a future distinct from each other; the two first only being *certain* as having existed, the last being still contingent upon the divine will. It is only from his knowledge of what that will *will be* that even God can be certain as to the future. We must also conceive the divine Mind to be susceptible of satisfaction (if we may use the expression) in the evolution and working-out of his plans, and, in so far, of being influenced and acted upon by what we may term external causes.

Now, why may not prayer in itself be one of these causes? May not the perception of the earnest desire of the creature be a cause acting upon the divine Mind (we need scarcely say that it is only the thoroughly earnest and sincere prayer which is entitled to the name)? And may we not go a step further, and say that every prayer becomes one of the endless series of *events*, and so *must* have an *effect?* — what, or in what way, is beyond us to know. That the Creator foresaw that such cause would arise, need not diminish its influence when it actually arises. It seems only reasonable further to conceive, that, according as prayer emanates from a mind more or less in harmony with the divine Mind, so we may anticipate that the effect will correspond.

I am, sir, &c.

W. Y.

THE EFFICACY OF PRAYER.

[TO THE EDITOR OF "THE SPECTATOR."]

SIR, — Owing to my absence from England on a somewhat erratic tour, I have only just received "The Spectator" of the 3d and 10th of this month, — the first containing your article on the "Efficacy of Prayer," in answer to Mr. Galton; and the second, several letters on the same subject. I hope it is not altogether too late for one more, as there is an aspect of the question which has not been touched upon by the others, which I am very anxious to bring before your readers, as affording the only ground on which belief in the efficacy of prayer can be held consistently with the belief in the invariable order of Nature, which is from year to year extending and strengthening its hold upon all educated minds. Prof. Tyndall, Mr. Galton, and all other scientific opponents of the former belief, of course, direct their efforts to show that prayer is inefficacious over the course of physical events, and obtain an easy success; first, because, even in cases of apparent physical changes in answer to prayer, it is impossible to prove that they were not mere coincidences; and, secondly, because their opponents have, unconsciously, it is true, but not the less surely, as little belief as themselves in the power of prayer to alter the order of Nature, where that order is known and manifest. The most devout believer in prayer would never, in our day, dream of praying that the sun should be arrested in its course, though the fate of all that was dearest to him on earth depended on the prolongation of the day or night. The habitual and lifelong experience of the invariable order of the sun's course would be too strong, and the consequent perception of the magnitude of the miracle required to change it, too vivid, to allow the idea of praying for it even to enter the mind. It is clear, that, in every case where the same certainty of experience existed, the same sense of the inutility of prayer would follow; and that the only real difference between the scientifically educated and the uneducated mind in this matter is the extent of the range of phenomena in which respectively they perceive and feel the immutability of natural order. Were the laws of meteorology, or those which govern disease, ever to become so thoroughly and universally known as to form part of the habitual experience of mankind, people would no more pray for health or fine weather than they pray now for the sun to halt on its way. They would instinctively recoil from the arrogant absurdity of asking that a miracle involving changes in the settled order of the universe should be worked for their special benefit, which might be the special disaster of their neighbors. Even now, I believe, the feeling once expressed by the late Duke of Cambridge, when prayers for fine weather were being read in church, — "Very proper, very proper; but it won't come till the wind changes," — is that of most modern congregations; and few forms of scepticism are more destructive of true religious faith. There is another and far higher ground than any possible or probable increase in our scientific knowledge, which will lead to the disuse of prayer for physical boons, *i.e.*, the higher conception of God, which grows with the growth of moral and spiritual life, — the conception of him as a perfectly wise and good Father, to whom we stand in the relation of weak, blind, and helpless children, superseding the conception of an omnipotent Autocrat, whose wrath may be propitiated, or favor won, by the gifts, prayers, or praises of the slaves of his arbitrary will. The mind to which the former conception has become a reality revolts from the ineffable arrogance and folly of petitions which would dictate to that perfect goodness, and alter the order established by that perfect wisdom. There can be but one prayer with reference to the outward events of life, for him who has faith in God as his Father and King: "Thy will be done; give me strength to do and bear it." And here we come to the prayer which is efficacious, to the domain in which prayer is all-powerful, and never fails of its answer; and that answer is not a matter of belief, but of knowledge. He who has prayed in agony of soul, every fibre of his being quivering with dread of the cup presented to his lips, *knows* that his prayer is answered, when the angels of strong patience and enduring faith descend into his heart, ministering the peace of perfect trust till he can take the cup with unfaltering hand, and drain it, saying only, "Thy will, not mine, be done." He who, in the dark storm of doubt or temptation, has prayed for light, only for light to see the truth and the right, *knows* that his prayer is answered, when a path becomes visible in which he is constrained to tread, let it lead where it may. And, when we pray like this, we know that we cannot pray amiss. There is no earthly blessing which may not be a curse in disguise; but faith, love, purity, strength to do our duty even unto death, these must ever remain blessings, the value of which cannot change with any change of circumstances. Those, again, to whom prayer "is not only petition, but communion," — they, also, know that their prayers are answered, when in the stillness of morning or evening, in the hush of midnight, or the pause in the toil and turmoil of the day, they lift up their hearts to that Presence whose holiness shames all impurity, whose love shames all selfishness, whose ceaseless activity shames all faint-hearted sloth. To tell all these that they first imagine the strength, the light, the help, they are conscious of receiving, and then account for them by imagining a God who answers prayer, is neither a more nor less valid argument than to say that we first imagine the impressions we are conscious of through our senses, and then invent an external world to account for them. The proof of the existence of a God in communion with the souls he has created is of precisely the same kind as the proof of an external world, and is equally incapable of being demonstrated or disproved.

The question of the efficacy of prayer for the moral welfare of others — family, country, or race — is not so easy to deal with. We can have no *knowledge* that changes we have prayed for in other minds are really the results of our prayers. One result we can, indeed, reckon upon; for he who prays in spirit and in truth for the good of others will do all that in him lies to promote it: and in this way a prayerful people — I do not mean a people who say their prayers — will so far bring about the fulfilment of their own petitions. All other means by which such prayers become efficacious are hid from us in impenetrable mystery. This only is certain, that no instinct is stronger than that which impels us to pray for those we love, — impels even those who never pray for themselves, and have no conscious belief in a God who can hear and answer prayer. Such an instinct, so powerful, and so universal, carries with it, to all who believe in a beneficent Creator, its own proof that it cannot have been implanted in vain, a miserable mockery of the unselfish affection which is the divinest thing within us; and beyond this the understanding cannot go.

I am, sir, &c.

M. G. G.

CHAMOUNI, Aug. 22, 1872.

[This letter must close this correspondence. — ED. "SPECTATOR."]

THE DISCUSSION ABOUT PRAYER.

A FEW remarks, in conclusion, on the very remarkable correspondence which we have published, and which we have suppressed, — mere considerations of space have compelled us to suppress many times as much as we have published, including some very able letters, — concerning the efficacy of prayer, may, perhaps, bring out the opposite views taken by the scientific and by the religious mind of this generation, with more clearness than was possible when it began. In the remarkable paper by Mr. Galton, which recommenced the discussion, there were two main threads of the argument. First, Mr. Galton, with happy results for his own case, —

though in perfect conformity with the true statistical spirit, which always, and quite rightly, endeavors to get free of the error likely to result from studying individual instances, and to test general laws by large averages, — appealed to the results of *formulated* prayers for the life of kings, for the grant of grace, wisdom, and understanding to the nobility, and so forth, and showed by figures that those prayers are by no means answered by any special lengthening of the life of sovereigns, and appear to be explicitly rejected as regards the wisdom of the nobility, since insanity — a characteristic the most opposite to "grace, wisdom, and understanding" — is commoner in their caste than in most others. And Mr. Galton made a strong point of the lives of missionaries. There, he very fairly said, if anywhere, you would be sure that the ground of the prayer for length of life is eminently rational and disinterested. A great part of a missionary's life is spent in acquiring a thorough command of the means of communicating with the people he is to convert. Yet missionaries die, like other men, from the effects of climate, before they have even brought their devout purposes to bear on the people they address. Even if they do not, there is no supernatural lengthening of their lives. Their averages of life are not unlike the averages of profane lives. They, as a class, appear to owe nothing to their religious purpose, or the prayers for a long career, which their religious purpose may be supposed to occasion. Such was his first point; and it is only fair to add that he did not assume, but carefully repudiated, any abstract ideas of physical law as bearing on these questions. He was candid enough to point out, — what some of our correspondents, who otherwise take Mr. Galton's view, have forgotten or ignored, — that, apart from the supposed invariability of physical laws, many means are open to the Christian's Providence of answering such prayers as these through the mere exertion of influence over the *minds* of the missionaries, or other subjects of the prayer. God may keep a man out of peril of tropical fever, or wreck, or assassination, by simply so guiding his thoughts and purposes as to restrain him from exposing himself to the conditions or causes of these dangers. If he does not so guard us, it is not from any want of purely spiritual resources for so doing. Mr. Galton's second point was, that there is quite enough to account for the universal use of prayer, and for the relief it gives, without supposing that prayers are answered. The germ of feeling, he said, which leads to prayer, is common to the lower animals, especially to mothers which have lost their young. "There is a yearning of the heart, a craving for help," he said with a good deal of eloquence and pathos, "it knows not whence, certainly from no source that it sees. Of a similar kind is the bitter cry of the hare when the greyhound is almost upon her. She abandons hope through her own efforts, and screams — but to whom? It is a voice convulsively sent out into space, whose utterance is a physical relief." And he added, in a subsequent letter printed in these columns, that prayer is in no other sense than this intuitive with men; and that it acquires the apparent character of an imperative instinct, only through the ascendency of a habit early implanted by the piety of mothers, or other friends and teachers.

To Mr. Galton's arguments, it has been replied by ourselves, or some of our correspondents, that there is no real basis such as Mr. Galton is so eager to assume for a statistical treatment of the results of prayer; since, in the first place, prayers are not mere utterances in the vocative case, of which any specimen is as good as another, but vary in proportion to the depth and intensity of the life thrown into them; so that the very kind of prayers by which chiefly Mr. Galton tests his case — the formulated prayers for *classes* of persons — are, probably, those which partake least of all of the spiritual essence of prayer. Again: we might have added that the general prayers in question are not exclusive prayers, the efficacy of which, if they have efficacy, implies that the classes named shall have *longer* lives than other people, — since *all* classes are successively included, all "the sick" and all "the afflicted," until we reach the comprehensive prayer for "all thy people," —but, on the contrary, they are mere classifications to help the imagination of the petitioner; in other words, are prayers which would be answered rather by the greater health, bodily and mental, of the whole people, than by any comparative favor to a particular section of them. Further, it has been replied, that, the intenser and the truer is the spirit of any prayer, the more completely is a prayer offered in that spirit wholly outside the reach of classificatory observation, and the less would it prescribe to God the exact mode in which it should be answered; so that, even if it could be observed and classified, it would be hard indeed, without cross-examining him who offered it on the deepest secrets of his spiritual life, to determine whether it had been answered or not. Finally, we have observed that the only prayer which we know to have been offered throughout all the ages of the Christian Church, from the depth of the Christian heart, — the prayer for the progress of Christ's gospel, — has been granted in the most marvellous way, and that against all the *a priori* probabilities of the case, if there were no God who answers prayer. In relation to Mr. Galton's second thesis, — that though prayer, so far as it is a blind cry of nature for help, directed it knows not whither, may be intuitive, yet so far as it is a conscious spiritual address to a perfect and all-powerful invisible Being, it is a result of the education (we use the word in its highest and truest sense) of complex faiths and affections, — there is, we think, a very general disposition to agree with Mr. Galton; and we confess that we do not see the bearing of this part of his argument on his sceptical position. His drift appeared to be, "Do not argue that prayer, in your sense, is inseparable from the higher nature of man. The mere blind cry for help may be inseparable from that nature; but the belief in the reality of that help depends on the special line of development of the intellectual and moral life." To which we reply, "that, of course, so far as the blind cry for help is not naturally and essentially connected in man with the sense of right and wrong, with the transcendent obligation of doing right, and the need of getting grace to do it, so far, certainly, intellectual development may fail to give this blind cry any more certain object than is present to the lower animals in the agony of their death-spasm; but, in our opinion, the normal development of the emotion which sends this instinctive cry into the night for help is bound up with the growth of moral law within us, and with the growing faith in the grace and love of a Law-giver." On this last point, the believers in prayer are, no doubt, at issue with Mr. Galton, but not many of them, as far as we can see, on the point which he presented to us. If disbelief in a God who can give, at the very least, ample moral power in answer to earnest appeals for it, — and with it the many physical gifts of which such moral power may be the source, — is a natural and normal result of the accumulation of experience, inward and outward, then Mr. Galton's position as to the "intuitive" origin of prayer comes to something. If not, not.

It will be observed, that, in this account of the opposite positions taken by Mr. Galton and by his opponents, we have excluded the somewhat irrelevant discussion, carefully excluded also by Mr. Galton himself, as to the *means* by which God may answer prayer without miraculous interference with natural laws. We may fairly assume that no modest Christian will pray for a miracle for his own particular benefit, or that of his friends, — *i.e.*, for any interference which would unsettle all other men's confidence in the great invariable laws known to us, and therefore their trust in the God of Nature, — nay, even that he could hardly believe it permitted to a religious mind so to pray. But it does not follow from this at all that it is permissible to pray for spiritual blessings only. How any clear-headed man can doubt, that, if we are to assume any scope for a real answer to prayer at all, it can be strictly limited to spiritual blessings, we cannot see. If God gives what is best for us independently of all prayer, then to pray for even spiritual blessings is quite superfluous, except on the dishonest theory of re-acting upon yourself by a kind of dramatic spiritual fiction. If, as all who believe in prayer suppose, he has, for the sake of securing free communion between himself and his creatures, thought right to leave many good things ungiven till they are asked for from the bottom of the heart, in an act of free intercourse with himself, then, though good men will always suspect their prayers for happiness and the supposed means of happiness much more, and offer them much more submissively, than their prayers for goodness, it seems to us impossible to say that it is wrong or useless to include them in their prayers. As to God's conceivable power of answering such prayers without miracle, Mr. Galton himself points out how wide and close is the interweaving of the physical and spiritual, so that, to an all-powerful Being, it is hard to conceive what even physical ends might not be gained by mere action on the spirits of men. If, for example, as some sober observers believe, — we are not implying any belief in it ourselves, but putting a mere hypothesis, — even heavy physical objects can be raised, and serious physical ailments cured, by new forms of purely "psychic" force, it would not be in the least inconceivable that the climatological causes of rain itself might be controlled without "miracle" by the agency of prayer. At all events, we certainly know far too little of the interweaving of spiritual with physical laws to dogmatize about the impossibility that God should answer earnest and humble prayers for even physical blessings without miracle. Undoubtedly, however, the whole strength of the belief in prayer centres on that conscious and imperious need of man for spiritual and moral help, which makes prayer to the Source of all righteousness a vital function of his inner life, — a need which may often justify, and oftener excuse, the prayer for physical blessings, such as the life of those dear to us, or even much meaner things, so far as these seem really bound up with the deepest needs of the spirit.

It will be said, with perfect truth, that this review of the controversy with Mr. Galton only comes to this, — that while his statistical argument against the efficacy of prayer goes for very little, or, to give our own true valuation of it, for nothing, the argument on our own side, being merely *a priori*, has no force for those who look at the matter, as Mr. Galton does, as a mere case for impartial investigation by the methods of inductive science. And this we freely admit. We utterly deny that all truth is attainable by the same avenues. We do not doubt that Mr. Galton could disprove the "efficacy" of (human) love quite as successfully (or unsuccessfully) as the efficacy of prayer. We feel little doubt, for instance, that beautiful faces have, on the whole, attracted to themselves more love, both at home and abroad, than homely faces; and, very likely, Mr. Galton could prove beyond all doubt that the owners of beautiful faces have reaped from the love thus lavished upon them much more anguish and calamity than joy. If, however, Mr. Galton were to argue from this that human love has no "efficacy" to shed gladness on human life, the common sense of mankind would probably laugh him down, and declare that this was not a region in which, at present at least, statistical methods can be applied with any kind of advantage. We say the same of the argument against the "efficacy of prayer." Apart from the *a priori* scientific preconceptions which Mr. Galton himself disowned, but which constituted all the real attraction of his argument for the great majority of those who eagerly seized upon it, the statistical method has just as much applicability to the question of the "efficacy of prayer," as it has to the question of the efficacy of the human affections to produce happiness, — in other words, none at all.

VIII.

THE FUNCTION OF PRAYER IN THE ECONOMY OF THE UNIVERSE.

BY REV. WILLIAM KNIGHT, DUNDEE.

"CONTEMPORARY REVIEW," VOL. XXI., JANUARY, 1873, PP. 183–189.

THIS article was made the occasion of the discipline of Mr. Knight by the Free Church Presbytery of Dundee, of which he was a member. He had previously been tried by the same presbytery on charges preferred against him for preaching, on invitation, in the Unitarian chapel in London, of which Rev. James Martineau was minister.

Mr. Knight was censured by the Church court for the view of prayer here presented. In consequence, he withdrew from the Free Kirk; and St. Enoch's Church, of which he was minister, followed him. They joined the Established Presbyterian Church of Scotland, action being taken by the General Assembly in his favor, and he and his church were formally received by the Dundee (Established) Presbytery, June 10, 1874.

VIII.

THE FUNCTION OF PRAYER IN THE ECONOMY OF THE UNIVERSE.

RECENT controversy regarding the function of prayer in the economy of the universe has illustrated the almost chronic tendency of two schools of thought, and the seemingly inveterate bias which they produce. The reluctance of the religious world to admit that there is a sphere to which prayer (in the sense of petition) is inherently applicable, is quite as conspicuous as is the hesitation of the physicist to concede its legitimacy, and to admit its power within the spiritual domain. It is natural that those whose life-work is the investigation of physical law, and whose researches are rigorously governed by the methods of induction, should wish to prove the value of an alleged power by definite experimental tests, such as the collection of statistics, or by some process not inferior in accuracy to those on which all science rests. But it is manifestly unfair to deal thus with a power which the wisest of their opponents remove altogether from the sphere of physical causation. It is, perhaps, equally natural that those whose deepest experience records that prayer "availeth much," should shrink from narrowing the area to which its efficacy extends, and, perceiving that the spiritual and physical forces are interrelated and reciprocal, should be jealous of any encroachment from the physical side. But it is as unphilosophical for the spiritualist to thrust within the province of the naturalist a power which is unchallengeable within its own sphere, as it is for the naturalist to slight a force the *rationale* of which escapes his physical tests.

The controversy resembles that which has lasted from the dawn of speculation between the intuitionalists and experimentalists; in which the disciples of both schools are reluctant to concede the full value of the data in which the counter-theory takes its rise. It is, indeed, but a subordinate phase of the same controversy, kindred, in this respect, to that which divides the advocates of evolution from those who believe in successive incursions of creative force. The success which has attended the labors of naturalists in accounting for the origin of species by "natural selection," has induced them to extend the operation of the law to the intellectual and moral nature of man, where (though it explains subordinate phenomena), in the presence of free-will, it breaks down. While the discussion is exhilarating, and the whole controversy a stimulus to patient and accurate research, *collision* between the two schools is philosophically illegitimate, and fruitless of result. In the one system, we see the spiritual protest of the reason and the conscience against the domination of material law and the paralyzing sense of necessity, but, in alliance with it, a frequent vagueness of statement, the airiness of mysticism, and occasionally an indifference to facts. In the other, we experience the healthful recoil of the scientific mind against all rash ontology, and alleged but unverifiable data, but, along with it, the frequent collapse of that spiritual instinct which leads behind the barriers of physical sequence. It is the part of a wise eclecticism to attempt a reconciliation between the opposite schools, and, in the question at present brought to the front (the validity of prayer), to vindicate against the physicist its function in the economy of Nature, and, against the ultra-spiritualist, to maintain the invariability of natural laws, and the irreverence of human entreaty for any interference with these. It is a blot upon our civilization, that, in the conduct of this controversy, there has been so much heat and acrimony, and a lack of comprehensive fairness on either side.

No one, even slightly acquainted with scientific methods and results, can, for a moment, brook the idea of any interference with the laws of external nature produced by human prayer. We may add, that (be our knowledge of science virtually *nil*) we can scarcely doubt that the amount of physical force within the universe is incapable either of increase or diminution, but only of endless modification; that the physical nexus between phenomena, in their ceaseless flux and reflux, is never broken; while the order in which the phenomena appear is governed by the rigor of adamantine law. The links of the chain of physical sequence continue to lengthen out interminably, connecting the past with the present, and uniting the present to the future infallibly. Catastrophe, the breaking of the chain, is simply inconceivable. And, so far as we can think of the complex economy of Nature as a series of pre-arrangements, they have been adjusted each to each with the completest mastery of all possible emergencies. Were they ever altered at the suggestion of a creature, either they were imperfect before the suggestion was made, or they were made less perfect by means of it. If previously perfect, the change would be undivine; and, if not perfect until the change, we could with difficulty believe in the perfection of Him who made it.

This conception of the absolute fixity of physical law is one which the progress of science has made axiomatic. Belief in an all-comprehending Intelligence, which saw "the end from the beginning," and "determined beforehand" the history of every inorganic atom, and the evolution of each sentient structure, is a postulate of rational theology; and that, in the guidance of the universe, its great Superintendent acts according to laws "set up from everlasting" is no less axiomatic. The more vehement opponents of this doctrine boldly challenge the datum from which it starts; viz., the invariability of material law. They say that it is an unproved, and, therefore, an unscientific assertion; that the sequences which seem to us invariable are so necessarily. Let us grant that the invariability is not "in the nature of things." The calm rejoinder of the physicist is, "We have no scientific experience to warrant the belief that Nature's sequences ever *are* variable;" and, mere experience taken as our guide, the solution of the question on both sides would be easy. The efficacy of prayer to quicken and exalt, to change the character, and elevate human life, is a fact of consciousness. On the other hand, we have, now-a-days, no instance of the suspension of physical law in answer to prayer. Alike in the physical and moral region, the causal nexus is inviolate. In both, it is always as a man sows, that he reaps. If he injures his physical frame, he reaps the consequence in physical detriment: if he impairs his moral power and spiritual vision, he gathers the harvest of moral degeneracy. But there is no confusion of the spheres of moral and physical agency. To put it otherwise, a spiritual antecedent will not produce a physical consequent. The exercise of the religious function of prayer cannot directly effect any material change. It is the appeal of spirit to spirit, conducted within the spiritual sphere, for purposes that are strictly supra-natural.

It is vain to reply that we are continually interfering with the seemingly fixed laws of the universe, and altering their destination by our voluntary activities, or scientific appliances; for, in all such cases, we simply make use of existing forces. We are ourselves a part of the physical cosmos; and, in accordance with its laws, we exert a power which changes external nature. But we can never escape from the domain of law. Our act, were we to attempt it, would itself be a link in the chain of phenomenal sequence. The very moment we put it forth, as agents in a phenomenal world, that instant the energy we exert (itself determined by prior influence) enters as a new element into the vast chain of physical causation. In short, we can only change the existing order by the exercise of a power which is itself a part of that order, and whose every movement is regulated by law.

The extremely vague manner in which those who imagine that prayer can directly alter the sequences of Nature state their case, is in the last degree unscientific. Thus it is said, May not God, who is sovereign and free, direct the forces of Nature in one direction rather than another, in reply to the free entreaty of a creature whom he encourages to pray? and the atmospheric phenomena are supposed to be peculiarly amenable to such "direction." Suppose, then, that, after a period of dry weather, prayer is offered, and rain begins to fall, will the theologian venture to deny that there was as exact an order in the physical antecedents as there would have been, had no prayer been offered? Will he hazard the assertion, that there was a break in the nexus between the descent of the rain and the physical causes which produced it; that a spiritual agency, exerted by the petitioner, has become the cause of the atmospheric change (the condensation of the cloud, and the descent of the rain) at a particular spot and a special time? The crude notion seems to be widely entertained, that because the changes of the weather are apparently capricious, the wind blowing "as it listeth," it may be sent forth on special errands in answer to human entreaty. Is not this the polytheistic notion of Eolus, with the winds in his fists? It is supposed that the destination of a physical force can be arrested, and the otherwise inevitable result prevented, by an act of divine volition. But the antecedent *must* spend itself, and determine some consequent. It simply cannot be arrested, or lifted out of its place amongst the links of physical causation, without the whole chain falling to pieces. Its efficiency in giving rise to a new sequence *is involved in its very existence;* while the discovery of the correlation and transmutation of the forces proves that the prior agent is still present, and operative under an altered form.

But it is said, that, while the chain of physical sequence remains unbroken, the local *incidence* (if we may so speak) of each link may be determined by some ethereal wave of hyper-physical energy, transmitted along the entire line, from its fountain-head, in delicately subtle undulations, resembling the waves of light and sound, or the flash of electricity through a telegraph-wire; and that the course of this hyper-physical energy may be determined in answer to the prayers of man. This assertion has all the characteristics of an hypothesis devised to escape from the horns of a dilemma. It is not supposed to apply to the whole domain of Nature, but only to a part of it; since no one would pretend that the rotation of the seasons was thus determined. Yet the fluctuations of the weather between two seconds of time are as rigorously determined by law as are the larger successions of the seasons; and to imagine that the Supreme Power would thus isolate some physical events from the rest is inconceivable. It would introduce the most arbitrary casualism in place of the orderliness of law. Again: suppose that there be no physical "fountain-head," but an endless cycle of recurrent energy; and what becomes of the hypothesis? Further: what purpose would this hyper-physical wave subserve, that is not already and better accomplished in the ordinary causation of the universe? Again: the introduction of this casual element, overruling and deflecting some phenomena of Nature (much as the free volitions of a man determine the sequences of his acts), would infallibly disturb the rest, and introduce bewildering chaos. For, though hyper-physical in its origin and character, the effect it is said to produce is not hyper-physical (in that case we should have no controversy with its advocates), but physical; and it is believed to give rise to an interminable series of fresh physical results. That it should be in the power of any creature thus to launch a new agency almost at will into the pre-arranged system of Nature, and thereby to begin a series of changes which are absolutely interminable in their effect, is simply incredible. Lastly, we have no experimental evidence of this subtle wave of influence, or of its results, from which we might infer a cause. It is an unverified hypothesis at the best.

Setting it aside, therefore, we are forced to the conclusion that human prayer has no validity as a force directly working within the domain of physical nature. To pray for fine weather, or for rain (except as a humble expression of man's dependence upon forces that are vaster than he, and upon Him from whom they emanate), is quite as illegitimate as it is to pray against the approach of winter, the return of summer, or even against to-morrow's sunrise. If the rain we ask for is needful in our particular district, in the ultimate and general economy of Nature it will fall in due course. If it does not do so, it is simply because it, or its physical equivalents, have been required elsewhere in the balance of that supreme economy. To desire its local cessation when it seems excessive, or its local presence when there is a drought, is the mere impulse of human selfishness, anxious to possess the most desirable things in one's immediate neighborhood (and ignorant of what these really are), forgetting that the Administrator of the universe has to consider the greatest good of the whole number; that he is superintending the whole economy of Nature, in which the apparent bane of one district is the blessing of another, while *he* is devoid of favoritism; and that these terms, "bane" and "blessing," have really *no meaning* to the physical universe at large.

But we are repeatedly told by theologians that an answer to prayer within the physical realm is a sign of the divine presence, helpful to the suppliant's faith. Is this a worthy conception of God's relation to the universe, that he, every now and then, interferes with his established order to prove his own supremacy? that he interrupts the working of his machine, to prove that he is *there* behind it, and has *power* to alter Nature, or to grant the requests of his creatures? Is not such a notion the offspring of the very rudest anthropomorphism? It is difficult to imagine a poorer idea of divine revelation than is implied in such arbitrariness. To those who think it gracious condescension, it may be replied, that it would be quite as significant of caprice. It is supposed, that having created a tiny creature, and brought him into the midst of the universal order (a creature that scarcely ever comprehends the meaning of that order), the supreme Artificer finds it expedient continually to announce himself by an alteration of the course and destination of phenomena at the unenlightened (it may be the selfish) call of that creature, and that he does so while at the same time his presence is ceaselessly revealed within every pulse and movement of the universe. But the very purport of revelation (which is merely the withdrawing of a veil) is not to show the creature that primeval order *can* be violated, or that "the material is subordinate to the spiritual:" it is to announce the fact, that the spiritual lies abidingly *within* the material as its underlying essence. And, while this is the philosophical notion, is it not, also, the biblical idea of the relation which God sustains to the cosmos? We have no evidence that the writers of our sacred books regarded the power which manifested itself to them in unusual ways, as different from that of which we see a daily apocalypse in the material world. So far from this, these writers uniformly speak of all natural phenomena as the direct outcome of divine agency. God "walks on the wings of the winds," the clouds are "his chariot;" "his voice" is heard when it thundereth, and so forth. To the Hebrew prophets and psalmists, at least, the supernatural was the power which works *through* the natural order, of which all the forces of the universe are manifestations to men.

But there is a farther question to which the physicist may validly demand an answer. All men instinctively abstain from presuming to ask God for certain things within the physical sphere; for example, for constant daylight, for perpetual summer, for physical immortality, or for the resurrection of the dead. The physicist asks us, *Why* do we abstain from such requests, but because we find that they are contrary to the laws of Nature, that their occurrence would involve the absolute overthrow of the existing cosmical order? And he is equally entitled to press for an answer to the question, Why should we draw a line, and exclude *any* physical phenomena whatsoever from the category of the fixed and predetermined? By degrees we learn to include all that seems at first anomalous within the majestic sweep of predetermined law. And is it not in exact proportion to our ignorance of what is fixed, that we make it the subject of our petitions? Religious men do not pray for eternal sunshine or for physical immortality. Why? Simply because they recognize that such would be *contrary to the will of God as revealed in the laws of external Nature;* and it rests with them to prove that one single physical event may validly be excluded from the list of the predetermined, before they call on us to pray with reference to it. We are bound to reply to this appeal of the naturalist.

Meanwhile there is another objection that is fatal to this habit of prayer for things that are purely physical. It distorts the petitioner's idea of the moral character of God, leading him, almost invariably, to imagine that special catastrophes are signs of displeasure, calling for confession of sin, and repentance. A season of unusual cold and rain, resulting in a bad harvest and threatened famine; or a winter of prolonged storm, strewing our shores with wrecked vessels and wasted cargoes; or a time of cattle-plague; or an outbreak of cholera, — these are regarded as marks of the general displeasure of Heaven, calling for general confession of sin, and prayer for the lessening or removal of such disaster. Men do this, and yet call their ancestors irrational, because they prayed against eclipses, and the mediæval warriors foolish because they feared a catastrophe on the earth when the auroral light was colored in the sky. In both cases it is to cower with craven hearts as before a capricious Deity.

The habit of mind it induces is disastrous to piety and even to sincerity; and there is often mere arbitrariness, as well as spiritual unreality, in the appointment of humiliation days for bad harvests or the presence of a plague. It would be more rational to appoint a fixed hour for humiliation, to last the whole year round, for the thousand human miseries that are more acute and terrible than the loss of crops, or death of cattle, or winter wrecks, or the incursions of pestilence, can ever be. Even the most ignorant of those who observe such days do not regard the calamitous events as judgments for special sins. The divine words touching the Tower of Siloam have dissipated that idea, at least for Christendom. But it is judged expedient, when disaster overtakes a nation or a community, to make some confession of sin in general, and, in conjunction with it, to pray for the removal of the calamity. Now, so far as it can be obviated or lessened by human action, prudence, foresight, and conformity to the laws of Nature, man may validly pray to be enabled to put forth that foresight and sagacity, and to conform to these laws. But, in so far as the disaster is due to causes with which he cannot interfere, it is illegitimate in him to pray for their removal. His obvious duty, then, is to acquiesce in the will of the Supreme. If he prays as he should, it must be simply for the spirit of submission. Even in the former case, it is only indirectly that he may pray for the removal of a pestilence. He may ask for wisdom to cope with it, for a knowledge of the laws of health, and for ability to conform to these; inasmuch as unconscious aid is often vouchsafed to the will of the agent who is striving to observe them. Doubtless this is often involved in petitions for the removal of existing evil; but it is as commonly ignored in the selfish longing for some "special Providence" which may sweep the pestilence away.

But there is superficiality, as well as irreverence, in the easily-uttered cry for deliverance, which frequently dulls the edge of practical endeavor to remove the evil, and conform to the neglected law, expressive of the divine will. There is irreverence in it, implying a distrust of the absoluteness of the divine wisdom and love; and it is altogether irrational, if offered up in opposition to the clear evidence of experience that it is fruitless, and that God does not thus gratify wishes which may be the mere caprices of his creatures. Doubtless the undertone of all devout prayer is, "Not my will, but thine, be done;" that is to say, the petitioner confesses his ignorance of what ought to be, and rejoices in the surrender of his wishes. But, in addition to this acknowledged undertone, if God reveals the fact that his will *is* done *through the laws he has established*, is it not supreme irreverence in man, craving for a "sign and a wonder," to cry out for something more? It is blasphemous to imagine that God ever violates a law. The only violation of law of which we can form any conception is its *non-observance* by an agent who can and should obey it. And, in reference to that, he may always pray for strength patiently to conform to the eternal order.

Conceding all this (and that not reluctantly), because it is in conformity with the dictates of reason, and also with the "sweet reasonableness" of Christianity, we must also vindicate, against those who impugn it, the function and the no less "sweet reasonableness" of prayer, as a spiritual fact within the economy of Nature. It is unfortunate that our modern physicists do not begin their inquiry into the *rationale* of prayer by testing its value within the spiritual domain. They might disarm hostility to the doctrine they teach touching physical nature, were they to recognize in *spiritual* prayer, not a mere "potent supplement" to the religious life, but the very pulse of that life itself. Now, it is incorrect to say that prayer is ever regarded by its advocates as a "form of physical energy," unless as a loose figure of speech, that is simply a travesty of what is held by all rational theologians. Prayer is always believed (even by the most illiterate) to be a spiritual power, the exercise of which determines the acts of the spiritual Power above, which, in its turn, accomplishes a change amongst phenomena. This may be erroneous; and it is for the naturalist to combat it, if he is scientifically able to do so. But our physicists say they "cannot express their repugnance at the notion that Supreme Intelligence and Wisdom can be influenced by the suggestions of any human mind, however great." Is not this totally to deny the validity of prayer by an absolute assertion to the contrary? We are informed that modern science contends only for "the displacement" of prayer, not for its "extinction." But, when we ask what is the value attached to it within its own domain, we receive this very vague reply, "that in some form or other, not yet evident, prayer may, as alleged, be necessary to man's highest culture." It is a peradventure, at the best. It may be of use, and that only as a means towards "man's highest culture," and that in a way "not yet evident." Do the accumulated experiences of the ages, then, go for nothing on these points, — that the prayer of the righteous "availeth much;" that it is the opening of a window to the supernatural; and that, while a devout man prays, his spirit is touched from above to finest spiritual issues? Have all religious men who have prayed for inward light, quickening, and help, and believed that they were listened to, no claim to be heard as witnesses in favor of a fact which is dim to the scientific eye?

We maintain that the true spirit and function of prayer are purely spiritual (though, in one important respect, the *results* of prayer tend out beyond that region); and that it is in the spiritual freedom of man, on the one hand, and the eternal freedom of God, on the other, that we find its *rationale*. The being and the moral character of God, must, of course, be taken for granted in any discussion as to the function of prayer. To every theory of the universe that dispenses with his existence, or merges it in Nature, prayer is manifestly an excrescence. It might still be an impressive utterance of the soul in moments of sorrow, or tragic loss, or even of triumph, — like a stream chafing between the rocky barriers of its course; but it would have no rational ground, and could never be a duty. It is noteworthy, however, that the act of devotion arising out of the felt dependence of the creature is one of the means by which the latent sense of the divine presence may be quickened into life. Starting, then, with this postulate, — the existence and recognizability of God, — the *raison d'être* of prayer is almost self-evident. In a sense, it is by the avenue of prayer that we come unto God, even unto his seat. The act of devotion leads the worshipper into his presence, not as revealed in space or time, or through any representative form, but as the ever-present and eternal Life. It is but the inarticulate language of the heart, the voice of the spirit, recognizing its own original. This very power of recognition, however, implies superiority to the unconscious forces of the material world. Had we no free spiritual power within us, differentiating us from surrounding existence, we could not "*come into*" God's presence in the act of devotion; for surely, in that presence, man, as well as unconscious nature, always stands. But, endowed with intelligence and spiritual freedom, he may, by an act either of the will or of simple aspiration, present his spirit to the divine, withdrawing it from the sphere of the sensuous, and subjecting it to the influence of the supersensible. And the divine nature may then act upon the human to quicken and exalt, directly "endowing it with power from on high." In the conscious freedom of our own wills we recognize a power, irreducible by analysis, which proclaims our superiority to the links of physical causation, while it acts in unbroken harmony with these. It testifies, that, in our inmost essence, we are not the mere products of organizing force, but that we have (to use the Kantian terms) natures *noumenally* free, and therefore *noumenally* related to God. The sphere of prayer is, therefore, the life of the creature endowed with moral freedom and the capacities of spiritual growth. Its value to the individual consists in the impulse it conveys to the inmost energies of the soul in their ascent and progress. By a direct divine afflatus, it tends, when it is, in Pauline phrase, "prayer with the spirit and with the understanding also," to clarify the intellect, and to elevate the heart, to rectify the bias of the passions, to strengthen the conscience, and discipline the will, and to foster all the virtues. Are *these* results to be slighted, because the power which effects them is inoperative in external nature? In that outer region all is orderly and fair; but, in the region of the spiritual, there is conscious disorder, moral chaos, which is at once an evidence of the need, and a vindication of the reasonableness, of an interference with it. Since, then, it *can* be altered for the better (while physical nature cannot), and since the alteration of this internal world is accomplished by the efforts of a man's free will, while God works in it, and is impossible, in its highest phases, without help and co-operation from him, why should not man petition for that help? why should he not ask for the presence of the *Co-operator?* For that is absolutely all. Prayer involves petition; but it is request for nothing outward. The petition is but the expression of that hunger and thirst for the divine presence, of which the Hebrew psalmists write with such passionate ardors, — the longing for perfection, the desire to escape from fell disorder, and conform to the order of everlasting right, with absolute submission to the will of the Eternal. Thus the act of prayer is the very key to the kingdom of God. We cannot dispense with it without discarding all worship whatsoever, all recognition of the Supreme Being, or of "the power which makes for righteousness" in the world. If religion be the recognition of, and allegiance to, the personal and ever-present God, a man cannot be religious, and neglect devotion. He may be modest, reverent, humble, full of admiration, or awestruck before the mysteries and sublimities of the universe; but religious, in the sense above defined, he cannot be.

We are told, however, by all agnostic teachers, that this is a mistake; that the essence of religion is the recognition of mystery, the essential element of prayer being a feeling of wonder and admiration in presence of resistless force, unerring wisdom, and everlasting power. As our confidence in the eternal order deepens, we are lifted to the true "Rock that is higher than we;" and filial piety evidences itself by the absence of any wish for a change of that which *is*. Mute dependence on resistless force, fearing no catastrophe, believing in none, independent of all "means of grace" and seasons of devotion, — that is the *alpha* and *omega* of piety. Surely it is the old Stoic fate, with its one virtue of submission, under a roseate modern guise. To work and to wonder, — that, and that alone, is to pray. We are further told, that, whatever be the wisdom of the petitioner, his knowledge is literally less than nothing, and vanity, to the Most High; and that his ignorance, breeding humility, forbids every petition. In short, the more ignorant a man is, the more he will pray for; the more intelligent he is, the less he will pray for; and, when his intelligence is perfected, he will not pray at all.

It would conduce to clearness, and lessen the risks of misrepresentation, were we informed whether such a sweeping condemnation as the above applies to all petitions whatsoever, or only to prayer for physical well-being, and interferences with Nature. The opponents of prayer do not sufficiently recognize the fact, that very few, if any, petitions are offered up in an absolute and unsubordinated manner. Even when unaccompanied by the express reservation, "Thy will be done," this is (as we have remarked) the essential undertone, or suppressed premise, in all true prayer. It is the unvarying yet most musical refrain running through every song of devotion; and, if rash suggestions touching the physical world are occasionally heard from the lips of rude though pious worshippers, we may be sure that the Hearer of prayer, "unto whom *all* flesh shall come," does not despise the stammering speech due to infancy of mind. Such stammering, however, becomes irreverence in mental manhood; and in this matter, emphatically, when "we become men, we must put away childish things."

We have said that the mind trained in the patient study of Nature's processes learns gradually to include even seeming anomalies within the sweep of predetermined law; but, if trained also in reflective science, it asks, What constitutes "a law"? and discovers that it is but the expression of the way in which the forces of the universe fulfil their mission; and that is, in other words, to say, by which the eternal Mechanist and Sustainer works within his own creation. *He* is the living pulse within the whole machinery of Nature; and the laws of matter or of mind are but the indices of his activity, the generalized expression or interpretation of the way in which the supreme Artist, Builder, and Administrator, controls his own creation. So far all is fixed, though it is the fixity of unerring wisdom, unalterable, simply because it is the arrangement of an optimist Ruler. But, within the mind that contemplates this unchallengeable order, there is something that is not fixed. We are conscious of moral freedom, the autocratic power of self-determination, while we are also conscious of moral disorder, and the need of rectification. The latter consciousness impels the spirit instinctively to look beyond itself for aid; that is to say, it prompts it to pray; while the former suggests the presence of One who is the source of the freedom, and is able to re-adjust.

It is impossible, in this paper, to unfold the evidence which our moral freedom bears to its own Archetype and Original. But assuming the divine Existence, and the resemblance between the human and the divine, the corollary is evident enough. If within the fountain-head of the divine nature, in which the human lives and has its being, there is a fulness of life unexhausted in the existing universe, power in reserve, yet communicable, prayer is but the approach of the human spirit to its Source, that it may receive the inspiration of that power. We must admit the existence of this reserve of communicable life within the divine essence, unless we hold that it has exhausted itself in creation, or that the *moral* fountain-head is an exact counterpart of a *physical* spring, and that what issues from it previously entered it in an altered form; that is to say, unless we believe in the transmigration of souls, or their re-absorption in the universal life. But if an addition is made to the moral contents of the universe on the appearance of every new human life, there *must be* this reservoir of unexhausted power within the moral source. And, if it exists in eternal wealth and communicable freshness (its most spiritual features suggested by the wells of earth,—those "fountains and depths that spring out of valleys and hills"), man may surely pray for it, and may find it descend upon him, or, rather, rise up within him, pervading his faculties, moulding his life, and replenishing his will. Intelligent recognition of the ever-present Mind is itself an act of prayer. The expression of such power in the language of adoration or trust is secondary to the act of recognition itself. But no sooner does the soul look, as through a window (we must speak in material figures), on the supernatural, than desire to approach the divine Presence, and to be brought into harmony with it, instinctively arises. And that longing (of which St. Augustine has left so noble a record in his "Confessions"), the *desiderium* of the heart, is most truly the essence of prayer. It is petition for the loftiest order of good, tempered with submission, and yet prescient of success.

If, now, we are told by those whose researches have confined them for a lifetime within the tracks of physical law, that, with this region of "inner mysteries," they are unfamiliar, it might be a perfectly valid and strictly philosophical rejoinder, that they "have faculties within, which they have never used." If, recognizing the divine existence, they are not conscious of the stirrings of that instinct which prompts the prayer of the devout, of that flagging of the wing of all endeavor which evokes it in some, or that sense of loneliness which awakens the filial cry in others, they are not at liberty to treat it either as a weakness or an unproductive act, to be banished from the realm of scientific utilities. By the very conditions of the case, they are precluded from pronouncing on its validity, because they cannot isolate the phenomenon in question, throw it into a crucible, and subject it to analytic tests. It is simply impossible to bring the life of the petitioner within the compass of any experimental gauge. As has been well remarked, "we cannot enter into the heart of those who pray, and take scientific precautions lest the experiment be delusive, and measure what was the moral strength *before* the prayer, and what accession of strength has come *after* it" (F. Newman). Besides, the deepest aspirations of the soul are least discernible by those who study the process from without; and the most intense replies — accessions of spiritual power — are necessarily unperceived by those who merely watch the current in its flow, that they may compute the volume of its waters. They always reduce the worshipper to silence, and breed reserve. The soul may be kindled to unwonted glow with the inspiration of Heaven, and may find that the words of a litany, or the music of a psalm, are the fittest channel in which to express itself; but the power which has reached it from above can never be subjected to scrutiny in its origin or transit. The concession made by the physicist, that prayer may "strengthen the heart to meet life's losses, and thus indirectly promote physical well-being, as the digging of Æsop's orchard brought a treasure of fertility greater than the treasure sought," needs only to be extended a little farther in the same direction to warrant all we are contending for. If, along with the "wise passiveness" it breeds, helping us to bear the loss and the defeat, it becomes an active power, stirring the fires of devotion, and leading to moral victory, the immeasurable range of its influence will be conceded, and even a scientific truth discerned in that "counsel of perfection," *Ask, and ye shall receive.*

So far, we may not be challenged by any but the dogmatic materialist, or the necessitarian, or the agnostic. But we have already raised the question, Is there any thing beyond the life or subjective experience of the petitioner that may be legitimately sought in prayer? and have added, that, if the spiritualist maintains that there is, he is bound to define that thing, or class of things, with rigorous precision, and to show the reasonableness of his act. The character of the class in question is easily defined. It might be thought, that as the popular adage puts it, "Man's extremity is God's opportunity," the class would be that to which human efficiency does not extend. It is precisely the reverse. Whatever may be accomplished by human instrumentality within the physical domain may be a subject of petition, inasmuch as prayer may originate a movement which tends outward from the will of the agent, and indirectly accomplishes these results. This admission is in full consistence with our primary statement, that the sphere of prayer is wholly spiritual; for the area in which the answer is vouchsafed is the life of the petitioner (or of those for whom he prays), where the will of the Supreme may freely move the natures underneath its touch. Thus in asking for deliverance in a time of peril, the really devout heart will pray (though perhaps unconsciously), not for interference with existing order, but for help to enable it to conform to that order. And it may pray for the result, without alluding to the instrumentality; just as we set down a contraction, or a short-hand sign, for a full word.

To take two simple instances. We pray for a friend's life that seems endangered. Such prayer can never be an influential element in arresting the physical course of disease by one iota; but it may bring a fresh suggestion to the mind of a physician, or other attendant, to adopt a remedy, which, by natural means, "turns the tide" of ebbing life, and determines the recovery of the patient. Or we pray for the removal of a pestilence; and the answer is given within the minds and hearts of those who take means to check it or uproot it. The latent power that lies within the free causality of man may be stimulated and put in motion from a point beyond the chain of physical sequence; and crises innumerable may be averted through human prayer, thus dislodging a spiritual force that slumbers, and sending it beneficently forth from its "hiding-place of power." Nevertheless, it will always be exceedingly unsafe to infer, from the observation of results, that any such dislodgement *has* taken place. For, in the first place, there will always be a larger number of petitions offered up for recovery than are ever granted; and, secondly, there will be many more coincidences between prayer and recovery that have no *causal* connection. Restoration may begin immediately after prayer; but it would be extremely rash to infer that the former was a consequence of the latter. Suppose a case in which prayer is offered, and there is no subsequent interference by man in any way, and the patient recovers, it would be sheer assumption to affirm that the prayer had caused the cure. Even were it able directly to affect the physical chain of antecedents and consequents (which it is not), it would be impossible, in any single case, *to know that it had done so*. As in the case of spiritual response, we cannot insulate the phenomena one from another so as to apply an experimental test. There is manifestly no scope for inductive science to an invisible agency which eludes observation: therefore, we believe that answers to prayer touching things physical are only *possible* when effected through the agency and instrumentality of man; and even then, we can never know how far they have or have not been granted. It is easy to perceive the reason of this inability, and also to see the mischievous results which would ensue were such knowledge ours.

There is another aspect in which prayer for physical results may be regarded, though no reply is ever granted. It may be a legitimate expression of our *longing for perfection*, our desire for the harmony of creation, with the abolition of all that now seems to mar its order. It is doubtless a consistent theory, that, as we live in an optimist universe, there is now no real blot, or lack of harmony, within it; and that what seems imperfect is simply due to the nature of our lenses, or the limited range of the human eye, that cannot see all round the perfect sphere. It is more consistent, however, to believe that a real chaos exists, which will be but temporary; that its temporariness does not destroy its present reality; and that "the discords have rushed in," only that harmony may result. If, then, a disturbing element really exists, one who sees the meaning, and is attracted towards the universal order, may validly desire the extinction of its opposite, and may express that longing in a prayer. This, indeed, is the very essence of the cry, "Thy kingdom come: thy will be done in earth as in heaven." It is a prayer for universal harmony. The blight and pestilence of the world are surely abnormal: they are not a part of the absolute order, are not even the outcome of law. We cannot speak of the laws of disease as we speak of the laws of health. Disease is the non-fulfilment of the conditions of health: it is anarchic and lawless. It seems reasonable, therefore, to desire the extinction of disease and blight with physical discord of every kind, as well as to desire the abolition of all moral evils. The gradual wearing-out of an organic structure by slow decay, when it has fulfilled its function in nature, is no encroachment on physical perfection; but its removal by a sudden stroke we lament as untimely: though, in both cases, it is the same ending of terrestrial life; just as the plucking of a bud is a loss different in kind from the gradual decay of the flower when its bloom is over. And our desire for the physical perfection of the whole creation might prompt the expression of that longing to its Author.

But here, again, we are on the verge of rashness, and run the risk of inexactitude. It may be that the varieties of disease are as much a part of the fixed arrangements of the cosmos as are the different types of organization. Certainly the causes which produced them have worked for centuries, and must continue operative in the future. Their variety may have, also, a certain physiological beauty. It is more in keeping with the general plan of Nature that human life should terminate in a hundred ways than that all should reach old age, and fall monotonously into the tomb. Besides, we find a system of elaborate contrivances to inflict pain, and to effect slaughter and sudden death, in the animal world. The whole living system of Nature, from the infusoria to the mammal, is a storehouse of illustrations of the same apparent evil, while—

> "Nature, red in tooth and claw,
> With ravine shrieks against our creed."

And may it not be the best arrangement in our human world, that hundreds and thousands should die (as we say prematurely) to make way for successors, while their own life is continued elsewhere?

Thus, on the one side, the fatalist alternative meets us full in the face; and over against it are the signs of disorder, wreck, loss, pain, presenting us with a physical text, which we interpret as *disease*,—an element foreign to the perfection of the universe. We may refuse to be dragged either into the Scylla or Charybdis of this philosophical antinomy; but we can only do so by the recognition of a living Will ruling the universe beneficently. The Theistic faith and prayer do not remove the mystery that shrouds it; but they relieve its forward pressure.

History and experience alike testify that the power of prayer is simply immeasurable. Though to approach God with endless and irregular requests, soliciting him for favors, instead of arising to do his will, or acquiescing in it, is unquestionable irreverence, no theory of causation can rob the heart of its right to pray "without ceasing," or the intellect of its assurance that spiritual "prayer availeth much." Mutual concessions, such as those which often end the strife of rival litigants, are unknown in philosophical controversy; but it would promote a better understanding between fellow-workers in the cause of humanity, were our theologians and teachers of science to bestow upon each other a more frank, ungrudging recognition, and to say, as Aprile to Paracelsus, in Browning's noble drama,—

"Let our God's praise
Go bravely through the world at last:
What care through *thee* or *me*."

WILLIAM KNIGHT.

IX.

PRAYER. THE TWO SPHERES: ARE THEY TWO?

BY THE DUKE OF ARGYLL.

THIS was printed in the next (February) number of "The Contemporary Review," pp. 464–473, as an answer to Mr. Knight.

In a subsequent number of "The Review," Mr. Knight replied. His reply is a sharp criticism of the Duke of Argyll, and reiteration and amplification of the original argument in favor of two spheres for prayer. Mr. Knight endeavors to convict the duke of contradictions between some of his statements in "The Review" and statements in his "Reign of Law." As it advances nothing new in the argument, this reply is not deemed worth reprinting.

IX.

PRAYER.

THE TWO SPHERES: ARE THEY TWO?

MR. KNIGHT'S paper in the last number of this "Review" is an attempt to give a precise and logical definition to the function of prayer in the economy of the universe. This attempt is a bold one, and invites criticism. No one can deny that there are intellectual difficulties connected with the idea of prayer in its relation to "the determinate counsel and foreknowledge of God,"—difficulties, however, of exactly the same kind as beset all ultimate conceptions of our own free-will, and of its effects on the course of Nature. And, as regards the practical question of the fitting objects of petition in prayer, St. Paul expressly tells us, that "we know not what we should pray for as we ought."[1] If any new light can be thrown upon this subject, enabling us to define accurately what prayer can, and what it cannot, do, an important benefit would be conferred on the Christian Church.

[1] Rom. viii. 26.

Having read Mr. Knight's paper with close attention, I wish to indicate the grounds on which I think his attempt a failure, and his philosophy to be unsound. Not having time or opportunity at present to write more fully on the subject, I shall simply specify a number of propositions which are to be found in Mr. Knight's paper, either directly asserted, or by implication involved in various passages, with a few comments which suggest themselves upon each of these.

The first is, —

That there is a "sphere" to which prayer is "inherently inapplicable" (p. 221).

This is a very different thing from saying that there are some things, or many things, that ought not to be prayed for; as, for example, for things manifestly unreasonable. It involves the proposition that there is a particular class of things, capable of being accurately defined, for which we ought never, under any circumstances, to pray, not because we can see them to be unreasonable or wrong, but because, to them, prayer is inherently inapplicable. The next proposition gives us the definition. It is, —

"*Prayer is a power which is removed altogether from the sphere of physical causation*" (p. 221).

The difficulty in accepting this proposition is, that we are wholly ignorant how much the "sphere of physical causation" may include. If there be, indeed, two "spheres," absolutely separate, — the physical and the spiritual, — they are in such inseparable contact in (for example) our own organism, that we cannot in the least tell where the one begins, and the other ends. Many men are now in the constant habit of talking of thought as a "cerebration;" and they seem to regard this language as essential to a correct understanding of what thought is. There can, therefore, be no practical value in a definition which assumes an absolute separation where none such probably exists, where certainly none such can be proved, and the lines of which, even if it existed, cannot confessedly be traced. Strange to say, Mr. Knight's third proposition admits this, —

"*That the spiritual and physical forces are inter-related and reciprocal*" (p. 222).

If this be true, it does not seem quite easy to understand how the one is a sphere open to prayer, and the other is a sphere to which prayer is "inherently inapplicable."

"*That the application of the physical law of evolution (natural selection) to the intellectual and moral nature of man breaks down in the presence of free-will*" (p. 222).

This assumes that the free-will of man is not subject to law; or, at least, that it is not subject to law in the same sense in which physical nature is subject to law. My own conception of the sense in which "law" prevails in Nature is very different from the conception which Mr. Knight appears to entertain; but in this proposition we have the admission, that his conception of the "operation of law" is not applicable to the intellectual and moral character of man. This is important, considering what Mr. Knight's idea is of the "reign of law" in Nature, — an idea which is next explained to us in those loose rhetorical terms which are now so common on the subject, —

"*We can scarcely doubt that the amount of physical force within the universe is incapable of increase or diminution, but only of endless modification*" (p. 223).

This proposition, in so far as it represents any truth at all, has no relevancy whatever to the subject of prayer. There may be many excellent reasons why we should not pray for the stoppage of the earth's rotation; but even the success of such a petition as this would not involve the smallest addition to the amount of physical force in the universe. The arrested rotation would pass into other forms of motion. "Endless modification" of physical forces is all that is needed to satisfy even the most extravagant petitions.

Next we are told, that —

"*The physical nexus between phenomena in their ceaseless flux and reflux is never broken*" (p. 223).

If this means that there is always *some* physical tie between phenomena, it is (so far as we know) true, being simply one way (and a very obscure one) of expressing the general law of causation; but if it means that this law of causation is any impediment to will (divine or human) in working out its own designs, then it is not only untrue, but it is the reverse of truth. The constancy of elementary forces, and the certainty of causation, are the very conditions, and, so far as we know, the essential conditions, on which will works, and works with illimitable effect.

Next we are told, that —

"*The order in which phenomena appear is governed by the rigor of adamantine law*" (p. 224).

There is no intelligible sense in which this is true. The order of phenomena is capable of endless change. Plasticity, infinite plasticity, in the hands of knowledge and of power, is of the very essence of natural law in its combinations and results.

But, as Mr. Knight's idea of physical law is such as he describes it here, it is satisfactory at least to find that he admits the existence of an element in man which *breaks down* any attempt to apply to his "intellectual and moral nature" the same physical law which (he thinks) has been successfully applied to his body. The next proposition, however, seems to deprive this admission of all value, and even of all meaning. It is, that—

"*A spiritual antecedent will not produce a physical consequent*" (p. 225).

This proposition we know to be untrue in the case of our own organism. If we have a "moral and intellectual nature" separate from a mere physical nature, it is quite certain that moral and intellectual antecedents do produce physical consequents in our body, and, through our bodily action, upon external things. If, on the other hand, our "moral and intellectual nature" is *not* separate from our organism, what becomes of Mr. Knight's absolute separation between the two "spheres"? Again: if we are so much under mere "physical causation" that our spiritual antecedents can never produce a physical consequent, what becomes of Mr. Knight's former proposition, that we have, in any sense of the word, a free-will? Accordingly we find, that, in the next proposition, Mr. Knight gives up the doctrine of free-will altogether; for here it is,—

"*It is vain to reply that we are continually interfering with the seemingly fixed laws of the universe, and altering their destination by our activities or scientific appliances*" (p. 225).

If this be a "vain" reply to the materialist or the physicist who wishes to apply the ordinary law of physical causation to man's moral and intellectual nature, what other reply has Mr. Knight to give? What becomes of his previous assertion, that the attempt to apply to the mind of man the same physical law of evolution which has been applied to his body "*breaks down in the presence of free-will*"? and what becomes of a subsequent assertion, that the human spirit, recognizing in God its own original, "*implies superiority to the unconscious forces of the material world*" (p. 237)?

Next we come to Mr. Knight's reason for thus abandoning the position he had himself assumed, and for dismissing as a "vain reply" any reference to our own voluntary agency. The reason he gives is this, "*For, in all such cases, we simply make use of existing forces.*" No doubt: but how this should prove that a "spiritual antecedent will not produce a physical consequent," I cannot see. Have we, or have we not, a free-will, which enables us by a spiritual antecedent to make use of our own physical forces, and, through them, of other existing forces? Mr. Knight's next proposition seems to imply that we have not. It is this, —

"*We are ourselves a part of the physical cosmos*" (p. 226).

But if we are a part of the physical cosmos, *and nothing else*, then there can be no part of us outside the sphere of purely physical causation. If, on the other hand, we are part of the physical cosmos, but with an additional element whose working "*is a fact of consciousness*," then our being part of the physical cosmos does not show any "vanity" in quoting our voluntary agency as belonging to the separate "sphere" which Mr. Knight has endeavored to define and assert. Mr. Knight sums up some remaining sentences on the vanity of resting any argument on our own voluntary agency; thus, —

"*In short, we can only change the existing order by the exercise of a power which is itself a part of that order, and whose every movement is regulated by law*" (p. 226).

Here, again, we are landed in a mere confusion, or contradiction. If the power of will is a part of the existing order, it cannot properly be said to change it. But, if the power of will can change the existing order, it must be something more than a mere part of it. Or else the words, "the existing order" are mere words, and nothing more, capable of being made to mean any thing, or nothing, or every thing and nothing, alternately. And this I suspect to be very near the truth.

Next we take a sentence involving the following proposition: —

"*The destination of a physical force cannot be arrested, or the otherwise inevitable result prevented, by an act of divine volition*" (p. 227).

This proposition, it will be observed, involves not merely the assertion that physical forces cannot be destroyed or suspended by the Creator's will. Such an assertion would be bold enough; and I am quite ignorant of the scientific discoveries which entitle Mr. Knight to make it. But his assertion is much more stringent than this. As the *destination* of a physical force depends on its association with other forces of the same kind, and on the proportion in which it is so associated with one or more, the assertion of Mr. Knight, is that the divine Will cannot even *direct* physical forces to the accomplishment of particular ends. Man can do this to a limited degree, because he is part of the cosmos; but God cannot do it, although, I presume, Mr. Knight would admit that the subordination of the cosmos to God is involved in any idea of a Creator which we can form.

Next we have an observation to the effect, that the possibility of prayer affecting the physical sphere "*is not supposed to apply to the whole domain of Nature, but only to a part of it; since no one would pretend that the rotation of the seasons was thus determined*" (p. 228). This implies the argument, that the possibility of prayer being answered does not depend at all upon what may be called the reasonableness of the petition, and that a prayer for something which involves the ruin of a world is quite as absurd as a petition for something which (for aught we know, or for any thing that is probably true) may be done without any greater disturbance than is produced by any of our own actions in "changing the existing order." This argument is against common sense, and is obviously founded solely on the assumption, that the reasonableness, or unreasonableness, of a petition, has no bearing whatever on the possibility of its being granted; which possibility is absolutely negatived wherever any physical change is concerned, however small this change may be.

This proposition is accordingly distinctly formulated as follows: —

"*Yet the fluctuations of the weather between two seconds of time are as rigorously determined by law as are the larger successions of the seasons*" (p. 228).

This is quite true in one sense, and quite untrue in another. The sense in which it is true is, that all physical phenomena are the result of forces in combined operation, and can never be *uncaused*. The sense in which it is not true, is, that these combinations of force are incapable of direction, that they either never can be or never are changed. We know this to be false as regards man; and we may well decline to accept it as a self-evident truth with regard to God.

Next comes a sentence which shows that Mr. Knight again recognizes the analogy between the known agency of man and the assumed agency of a divine Will in changing the order of physical sequences. He compares the introduction of a "*casual element overruling and deflecting some phenomena of Nature*" with "*the free volitions of a man determining the sequences of his acts*" (p. 228); and he asserts that any such introduction "*would infallibly disturb the rest, and introduce bewildering chaos*" (*Ibid.*). Now, as this is not the necessary consequence of man's "interference," it is difficult to understand why it should be the necessary consequence of God's "interference," with physical causation.

Mr. Knight next tells us, speaking of the absurdity of praying for changes of weather, "*that the apparent bane of one district is the blessing of another;*" and that "*these terms, 'bane' and 'blessing,' have really no meaning to* (*in?*) *the physical universe at large*" (p. 229).

That what we mistake for banes may often be really blessings is very true, and ought always to be remembered. But that all we enjoy, and all we suffer, are given to us in measures absolutely fixed, and absolutely incapable of any other distribution than that which is determined by a purely physical necessity, has not been yet proved, or even indicated, by any fact of science or any analogy of Nature.

But then Mr. Knight farther tells us, that the purport of Revelation "*is not to show that the material is subordinate to the spiritual*," but "*to announce the fact that the spiritual lies abidingly within the material as its underlying essence*" (p. 230). But if this is so, if the spiritual is the very essence of the physical, how comes it that the two spheres can be so neatly and completely divided as Mr. Knight's fundamental proposition implies?

And yet, a little further on, we have a recurrence to this division and distinction as one which overrules all the possibilities of prayer. "*All men instinctively abstain from presuming to ask God for certain things within the physical sphere; for example, for constant daylight, &c. . . . Religious men do not pray for eternal sunshine, or for physical immortality. Why? Simply because they recognize that such would be contrary to the will of God as revealed in the laws of external nature; and it rests with them to prove that one single physical event may be validly excluded from the list of the predetermined* (p. 231). Here, again, the whole stress of the alleged impossibility is laid, not upon the moral character of a petition, but on its physical or non-physical character. Prayer is quite applicable in the spiritual, which is the essence of the material; but it is absolutely excluded in those outward physical forms which are the manifestations of the spiritual.

All this may be so; but it is not recommended to us by reason, nor (may I say so?) on adequate authority.

The difficulty of accepting it is not abated when we come to examine what Mr. Knight's idea is of the sole legitimate sphere of prayer.

Although God can not, or will not, alter physical sequences, man can do so, and ought to do so, as far as his means and his knowledge enable him. The sphere of his own action, therefore, and no other as regards physics, is the sphere of legitimate prayer. Mr. Knight says, "*Now, so far as it (calamity) can be obviated or lessened by human action, prudence, foresight, and conformity to the laws of Nature, man may validly pray to be enabled to put forth that foresight and sagacity, and to conform to those laws. But so far as the disaster is due to causes with which he cannot interfere, it is illegitimate in him to pray for their removal* (p. 233).

This involves the assertion that God never can or never does use any other agency than that of man to act upon physical causation. That God does use and bless human agency for the production of physical effects, and that the prayer for enlightenment, and for strength to use that agency well and wisely, is a legitimate, and ought to be an habitual, prayer, is no novelty among religious men. But that our prayers must cease when our own agency, or that of our fellow-men, is exhausted, is certainly a novelty. But, then, like many other novelties, "it requires confirmation." It does not commend itself to reason, or to science, or to any rational conception of the relations of a Creator to man and to the world, especially when the assertions upon which it is founded as an axiomatic truth are assertions which must inspire doubt as to prayer being available at all, even in the sphere which is assigned to it.

We have been told that a "*spiritual antecedent cannot determine a physical consequent.*" How, then, can the spiritual aid of God in the spirit of man determine, or help in any way, his physical exertions? And what if the physiologists should prove that man's "cerebrations" originate in his physical organization? how can the spiritual antecedent of the divine volition determine the physical consequent in the brain of man? I do not say that physiologists have been able to prove this; nor do I believe it to be capable of proof. But we all know that thought in man is so intimately associated with physical conditions, that they cannot be separated in the present world: and if we are to retain any belief in prayer at all, even in the spiritual sphere, it is not safe to be dependent on what may be found out, or what may be conceived, as to the nature and extent of this connection.

It is, indeed, satisfactory to find that Mr. Knight guards himself, or desires to do so, against this danger by the following emphatic declaration, "*In the conscious freedom of our own wills, we recognize a power, irreducible by analysis, which proclaims our superiority to the links of physical causation*" (p. 238). But it is idle to suppose that man's superiority to the links of physical causation can be successfully asserted when God's superiority to those links is denied. Mr. Knight has himself not only indicated, but has adopted, the bad metaphysics which pretend to make our supposed consciousness of free-will "reducible by analysis" to a mere delusion. We are ourselves parts only of the cosmos: all that is of us, and all that is in us, is itself determined by prior influence; and every movement which we think is "free" is in reality regulated by law. Men who have been deluded into the belief that words strung together after this fashion represent any truth whatever are not likely to be brought back to common sense by Mr. Knight's assurance, that "*the latent power that lies within the free causality of man may be stimulated and put in motion from a point beyond the chain of physical sequence*" (p. 246). For who knows how far this chain extends? Mr. Knight had previously told us, that "*the links of the chain of physical sequence continue to lengthen out interminably*" (p. 224). This may mean, either that the chain never ends, or that we do not know where it ends. If it never ends, there can be no point beyond it. If it does end, but we don't know where, then our prayers must not only be ignorant, but must be founded upon our ignorance, and upon that alone. Accordingly Mr. Knight, in another part of his paper, asks, "*Is it not in exact proportion to our ignorance of what is fixed that we make it the subject of our petitions?*" (p. 232). This, truly, is the result of Mr. Knight's theory; but it is not the result of the old Christian theory, or of any theory consistent with science, or our own experience. Mr. Knight's theory of a fundamental separation between the physical and the spiritual is a theory entirely unsupported by any evidence in observation or in consciousness. The spiritual, we have been told, is not superior to the material, but is only *within it*. Who knows, then, that the spiritual can be got at without passing through the physical as a crust, or an envelope, or as a channel? The thinnest bit of such a crust is enough, in Mr. Knight's philosophy, to intercept the divine power and will. He tells us, indeed, that "*the will of the Supreme may freely move the natures underneath its touch.*" But, then, no part of the chain of physical causation is among these natures; and any part of that chain extending beyond our knowledge will cut off our communication with God. It is in the face of our profound ignorance of the relation between the spiritual and the material, in the face of his own admission that the one underlies the other, and the one is the essence of the other, that Mr. Knight again tells the spiritualist — who believes that prayer can possibly affect any thing except the "*petitioner's own life and subjective experience*" — that he is "*bound to define that thing, or class of things, with rigorous precision*" (p. 245). This is, indeed, the great error at the root of the whole argument, — the assumption that we know what we do not know, that we can define what we cannot define, that our poor verbal distinctions reach and represent the real nature of things, instead of representing only one-sided aspects of them, and partial glimpses of a system only partially understood. Hence comes the use of language in senses inconsistent and self-contradictory, confounding the little knowledge we possess in empty and confused logomachies.

It is indeed difficult to understand how Mr. Knight could have penned the following very crude statement of the difficulty connected with the master-mystery, the origin of evil, and imagine that he is helping the definition of a legitimate sphere of prayer by dividing absolutely between the physical and the spiritual: "*So far as we can think of the complex economy of Nature as a series of pre-arrangements, they have been adjusted each to each with the completest mastery of all possible emergencies. Were they ever altered at the suggestion of a creature, either they were imperfect before the suggestion was made, or they were made less perfect by means of it. If previously perfect, the change would be undivine; and, if not perfect until the change, we could with difficulty believe in the perfection of Him who made it*" (p. 224). Can any one suppose that the "difficulty" here set forth can be confined to the sphere of "the physical"? And can any of us put these "difficulties" into words, without a perfect consciousness that we are talking nonsense, — talking about things which we do not in the least understand; so that it only remains to follow up such questionings with the confession, "So foolish was I, and ignorant: I was as a beast before thee"? [1]

[1] Ps. lxiii. 22.

The predominance of petitions purely spiritual among the petitions of the Lord's Prayer is a good argument for giving the same predominance to them in all prayer. But that great exemplar of prayer includes at least one direct petition for temporal blessings, and in all of them the two "spheres" are inseparably intermingled. Reason, science, and revelation alike point to the folly and ignorance of any attempt to draw an absolute line where we confessedly have not the knowledge to enable us to do so, and confirm the sound philosophy, as well as the piety, of the old Christian practice of "in all things making our requests known," with the overriding, overruling condition, "nevertheless not our will, but Thine, be done."

ARGYLL.

X.

PRAYER, THE CHARACTERISTIC ACTION OF RELIGION.

BY H. P. LIDDON, D.D., CANON OF ST. PAUL'S.

ONE of the Lent lectures by Canon Liddon, delivered in 1870, in St. James's Church, Piccadilly, London, and published, in 1872, in a volume entitled, "Some Elements of Religion," anticipates in substance, as well as in publication, the Prayer-Gauge debate, of which it forms no part historically. For that very reason it seems suitable to stand as the end, and wind up the discussion.

X.

PRAYER, THE CHARACTERISTIC ACTION OF RELIGION.

"Ask, and it shall be given you." — MATT. vii. 7.

RELIGION is the bond between the soul and God, which sin, by virtue of its very nature, breaks up and destroys. It is of importance to inquire whether man can strengthen and intensify that which he can, it seems, so easily ruin if he will. Does his power lie only in the direction of destruction? Has he no means of invigorating and repairing a tie, in itself so precious, yet, in some respects, so frail? The answer lies in our Lord's promise. Prayer is the act by which man, conscious at once of his weakness and of his immortality, puts himself into real and effective communication with the almighty, the eternal, the self-existent God. I say, effective communication; for prayer, as our Lord teaches in the text and elsewhere, is not without results. God answers prayer in many ways. His answers to the soul's petition for health and strength are collectively described as grace; grace being the invisible influence whereby he, on his part, strengthens and quickens the tie which binds the petitioner to himself. "Ask, and it shall be given you." Prayer, then, braces the bond of religion from the side of man; and grace, God's highest answer to prayer, braces it in a different, and far more powerful, sense, on the part of God.

It is not too much to say that the practice of prayer is co-extensive with the idea of religion. Wherever man has believed a higher power to exist, he has not merely discussed the possibility of entering into converse with such a power: he has assumed, as a matter of course, that he can do so. Upon desert plains and wild promontories, not less than in crowded thoroughfares and gorgeous temples, priesthoods and kings and multitudes have taken prayer for granted, as being the most practical, as well as the most interesting and solemn, concern of life. The surface of the earth, of parts of our own island, is still covered with the relics of some among these ancient worships. And if the implied conceptions of Deity were degraded, and the rites cruel, or inhuman, or impure, and the minds of the worshippers not seldom imbruted by the very acts which should have raised them heavenward, still the idea of worship as the natural correlative of belief in the superhuman was always there. To know that a higher Being existed, and interested himself, in whatever way, in the destinies of man, was to feel that it was at once a right and a duty to approach him.

And as we pass the historical lines within which, as

Christians believe, mankind has enjoyed a knowledge of God's successive revelations of his true self and his true will, we find that prayer is the prominent feature, the characteristic exercise, of man's highest life. Sacrifice begins at the very gates of Eden.[1] The life of early patriarchs is described as a "walking with God," a continuous reference of thought and aspiration to the Father above, who yet was so near them.[2] And after the Mosaic law was given, when the idea and range of sin had been deepened and extended in the mind of Israel, we find prayer organized in a system of sacrifices, suited to various wants and moods of the human soul, consciously dealing with its God as the king both of the sacred nation and of the individual conscience. Penitence, thanksgiving, intercession, adoration, each found an appropriate expression.[3] Later still, in the Psalter, prayer — the purest, the loftiest, the most passionate — took shape in imperishable forms. And when, at length, a new revelation was made in Jesus Christ, there was little to add to what was already believed as to the power and obligation of prayer, beyond revealing the secret of its acceptance. Our Lord's precepts[4] and example[5] are sufficiently emphatic; and his apostles appear to represent prayer, not so much as a practice of the Christian life, as its very breath and instinctive movement. The Christian

[1] Gen. iv. 4. [2] Gen. v. 24, vi 9. [3] Levit. i.–vii.

[4] Matt. vi. 9, xxvi. 41; Mark xi. 24; Luke xi. 2, xviii. 1, &c.

[5] Matt. xiv. 23; Mark vi. 46; Luke vi. 12, ix 28; John xvii. 1.

must be "continuing instant in prayer:" he must "pray without ceasing."[1]

1.

Each faculty, or endowment, or form of activity, that belongs to man has, over and above a number of more indirect effects, its appropriate and characteristic action, in which its whole strength is embarked, and in which it has, so to speak, its full play. To this law, religion is no exception. While its influence upon human life is strong and various, in proportion to its high aim and object; while it is felt, when it wields real empire, in every department of human activity and interest, as an invigorating, purifying, chastening, restraining, guiding influence, — it, too, has a work peculiarly its own. In this work it is wont, if we may so speak, to embark its collective forces, and to become peculiarly conscious of its direction and intensity. This work is prayer. Prayer is emphatically religion in action. It is the soul of man engaging in that particular form of activity which presupposes the existence of a great bond between itself and God. Prayer is, therefore, nothing else or less than the noblest kind of human exertion. It is the one department of action in which man realizes the highest privilege and capacity of his being. And, in doing this,

[1] Rom. xii. 12; 1 Thess. v. 17.

he is himself enriched and ennobled almost indefinitely. Now, as of old, when he comes down from the mountain, his face bears tokens of an irradiation which is not of this world.

That this estimate of the value of prayer is not universal among educated people in our day is only too notorious. If many a man were to put into words, with perfect honesty and explicitness, what he thinks, he would say that prayer is an excellent thing for a clergyman, or for a recluse, or for a sentimentalist, or for women and children generally; that it has its uses as a form of desultory occupation, an outlet for feeling, a means of discipline: for himself, he cannot really think that much prayer would help him much. It implies a life of feeling, perhaps, he would say, of morbid feeling; and he prides himself upon being guided only by reflection. It is sustained, he thinks, by imagination, rather than by reason; and he deems imagination puerile and feminine. His religion, whatever it is, has nothing to do with imagination, and is hard reason from first to last; and, accordingly, prayer seems to him to be altogether less worthy of the energies of a thinking man than hard work, whether it be work of the hands, or of the brains, whether it be study or business. The dignity of real labor is proverbial; but where, he asks, is the dignity of so sentimental an occupation as prayer? "For his own part, he thinks" (I am quoting words which have actually been used) "that religion is not worship, but only another name for doing good to our fellow-creatures."

Now, without saying one word to disparage the intimate connection between religion and philanthropy, let us examine the idea of prayer, which is taken for granted in such language as the foregoing. Is it true, that prayer is, as is assumed, little else than the half-passive play of sentiment, which flows languidly on through the minutes or hours of easy revery? Let those who have really prayed give the answer. They sometimes describe prayer with the patriarch Jacob as a wrestling-together with an Unseen Power, which may last, not unfrequently in an earnest life, late into the night-hours, or even to the break of day.[1] Sometimes they refer to common intercession with St. Paul as a concerted struggle.[2] They have, when praying, their eyes fixed upon the Great Intercessor in Gethsemane, upon the drops of blood which fall to the ground in that agony of resignation and sacrifice.[3] Importunity is of the essence of successful prayer. Our Lord's references to the subject especially imply this. The friend who is at rest with his family will rise, at last, to give a loaf to the hungry applicant.[4] The unjust judge yields, in the end, to the resistless eagerness of the widow's cry.[5] Our Lord's blessing on the Syrophœnician woman is the consecration of importunity with God.[6] And importunity means, not dreaminess, but sustained work. It is through prayer especially that "the kingdom of heaven suffereth violence, and the violent take it

[1] Gen. xxxii. 24. [2] Rom. xv. 30. [3] Luke xxii. 44. [4] Luke xi. 8.
[5] Luke xviii. 5. [6] Matt. xv. 28, 29; Mark vii. 28, 29.

by force."[1] It was a saying of the late Bishop Hamilton of Salisbury, that "no man was likely to do much good in prayer, who did not begin by looking upon it in the light of a work, to be prepared for and persevered in with all the earnestness which we bring to bear upon subjects which are in our opinion at once most interesting and most necessary."

This, indeed, will appear, if, looking to an act of real prayer, we take it to pieces. Of what does it consist? It consists always of three separate forms of activity, which, in the case of different persons, co-exist in very varying degrees of intensity, but which are found, in some degree, in all who pray, whenever they pray.

To pray, is, first of all, to put the understanding in motion, and to direct it upon the highest object to which it can possibly address itself, — the infinite God. In our private prayers, as in our public liturgies, we generally preface the petition itself by naming one or more of his attributes, — Almighty and Everlasting God! If the understanding is really at work at all, how overwhelming are the ideas, the truths, which pass thus before it! — a boundless power, an existence which knows neither beginning nor end. Then the substance of the petition, the motives which are alleged for urging it, the issues which depend upon its being granted or being refused, present themselves to the eye of the understanding. And if our Lord Jesus Christ is not him-

[1] Matt. xi. 12.

self, as being both God and man, the object of prayer, yet his perpetual and prevailing intercession opens upon Christian thought the inmost mysteries before the eternal throne. And thus any common act of real prayer keeps, not the imagination, but the understanding, occupied earnestly, absorbingly, under the guidance of faith, from first to last.[1]

Next, to pray is to put the affections in motion: it is to open the heart. The object of prayer is the Uncreated Love, the Eternal Beauty, — He of whose beauty all that moves love and admiration here is, at best, a pale reflection. To be in his presence in prayer is to be conscious of an expansion of the heart, and of the pleasure which accompanies it, which we feel, in another sense, when speaking with an intimate and loved friend or relative. And this movement of the affections is sustained throughout the act of prayer. It is invigorated by the spiritual sight of God; but it is also the original impulse which leads us to draw near to him.[2] In true prayer as in teaching, "out of the abundance of the heart the mouth speaketh."[3]

Once more: to pray is to put the will in motion, just as decidedly as we do when we sit down to read hard, or to walk up a steep hill against time.[4] That sovereign power

[1] Eph. vi. 18; John iv. 22–29; Rom. x. 14; Heb. xi. 6.

[2] Matt. xv. 8; 1 John iii. 21, 22.

[3] Matt. xii. 34; Luke vi. 45.

[4] John ix. 31; Matt. vii. 21; James iv. 7, 8. These passages all imply that prayer in which the will is not engaged is worthless.

in the soul, which we name the will, does not merely, in prayer, impel us to make the first necessary mental effort, but enters most penetratingly and vitally into the very action of the prayer itself. It is the will which presses the petition; it is the will which struggles with the reluctance of sloth, or with the oppositions of passion; it is the will which perseveres; it is the will which exclaims, "I will not let thee go, except thou bless me."[1] The amount of will which we severally carry into the act of prayer is the ratio of its sincerity; and, where prayer is at once real and prolonged, the demands which it makes upon our power of concentrating determination into a specific and continuous act are very considerable indeed.

Now, these three ingredients of prayer are also ingredients in all real work, whether of the brains or of the hands. The sustained effort of the intelligence and of the will must be seconded in work, no less than in prayer, by a movement of the affections, if work is to be really successful. A man must love his work to do it well. The difference between prayer and ordinary work is, that, in prayer, the three ingredients are more equally balanced. Study may, in time, become intellectual habit, which scarcely demands any effort of will: handiwork may, in time, become so mechanical as to require little or no guidance from thought: each may exist in a considerable, although not in the highest, degree of excellence, without any co-operation of the affections. Not

[1] Gen. xxxii. 26.

so prayer. It is always the joint act of the will and the understanding, impelled by the affections; and, when either will or intelligence is wanting, prayer at once ceases to be itself, by degenerating into a barren intellectual exercise, or into a mechanical and unspiritual routine.

The dignity of prayer as being real work becomes clear to us, if we consider the faculties which it employs. This will be made clearer still, if we consider the effect of all sincere prayer upon the habitual atmosphere of the soul. Prayer places the soul face to face with facts of the first order of solemnity and importance, with its real self, and with its God. And just as art, or study, or labor, in any department, is elevating, when it takes us out of and beyond the petty range of daily and perhaps material interests, while yet it quickens interest in them by kindling higher enthusiasms into life, so, in a peculiar and transcendent sense, it is with prayer. Prayer is man's inmost movement towards a higher power; but what is the intellectual view or apprehension of himself that originally impels him to move? Under what aspect does man appear to himself in prayer? In a former lecture, we have encountered the mystery which lies enclosed within each one of us, — the mystery which is yet a fact, — of an undying personality. It is that which each human speaker describes as "I." It is that of which each of us is conscious as no one else can be conscious. Its existence is not proved to us by a demonstration, since we apprehend it as immediately obvious. Its certainty can be shaken by no sophistical or destructive argument, since our conviction of its reality is based upon a continuous act of primary perception. No sooner do we withdraw ourselves from the importunities of sense, from the wanderings of imagination, from the misleading phrases which confuse the mental sight, than we find ourselves face to face with this fact, represented by "I." For it is neither the body which the real self may ignore, nor a passionate impulse which the real self may conquer, nor even that understanding, which, close as it is to the real self, is yet distinct from it. The body may be in its decrepitude; the flames of passion may have died away; the understanding may be almost in its dotage: yet the inward, self-possessed, self-governing being may remain untouched, realizing itself in struggling against the instincts of bodily weakness, and in crushing out the embers which survive the fires of extinct passions. Now, it is this self, conscious of its greatness, conscious of its weakness, which is the real agent in prayer. In its oppressive sense of solitude, even in the midst of multitudes, this self longs to go forth, and to commune with the Father of spirits who gave it life. This real self it is which apprehends God with the understanding, which embraces him with the affections, which resolves through the will to obey him; and thus does it underlie and unite the complex elements of prayer, so that, in true heartfelt prayer, we become so conscious of its vitality and power. It is in prayer especially that we cease to live, as it were, in a single faculty, or on the surface of our being: it is in prayer that we cease to regard ourselves as animal forms, or as social powers, or as family characters, and look hard, for the time being, at ourselves as being what we really are; that is to say, as immortal spirits, outwardly draped in social forms and proprieties, and linked to a body of flesh and blood, but, in our felt spiritual solitude, looking steadily upwards at the face of God, and straining our eyes onwards towards the great eternity which lies before us.[1]

Prayer is, then, so noble, because it is the work of man as man, — of man realizing his being and destiny with a vividness which is necessary to him in no other occupation. But what shall we say of it, when we reflect further, that, in prayer, man holds converse with God; that the Being of beings, with all his majestic attributes, filling and transcending the created universe, traversing human history, traversing each man's own individual history, is before him; that, although man is dust and ashes, he is, by prayer, already welcomed in the very courts of heaven? It is not necessary to dwell on this topic. Whatever be the daily occupations of any in this church, be he a worker with the hands, or a worker with the brain, be he gentle or simple, be he unlettered or educated, be he high in the State, or among the millions at its base, is it not certain that the nobleness of his highest forms of labor must fall infinitely below that of any single human spirit entering consciously into converse with the infinite and eternal God?

[1] Luke xviii. 13, 14.

2.

But granted, men say, the dignity of prayer, granted, even, its dignity as labor: what if this labor be misapplied? There are many functions in many states, very dignified, and not a little onerous, yet, in a social and human sense, not very productive. Is prayer, in its sphere, of this description? Has it no tangible results? Does it end with itself? Can the laborer in this field point to any thing definite that is achieved by his exertions?

The question is sufficiently serious at all times, but especially in our own positive and practical day. And it is necessary to make two observations, that we may see more clearly what issue is precisely before us.

In the first place, there is here no question as to the subjective effect of prayer, — the effect which it confessedly has upon the mind and character of the person who prays. Such effects have been admitted on the part of those who, unhappily, do not pray themselves; just as the Jews, at the time of the betrayal, were so alive to tokens in the disciples of companionship with Jesus. That all the effects of Christian prayer upon the soul, or most of them, are natural, a Christian cannot admit: he believes them to be chiefly due to the transforming power of the grace of God, given, as at other times, so especially in answer to prayer. But that *some* effects of prayer upon the soul are natural consequences of directing the mind and the affections towards a superhuman object, whether real or ideal, may be fully granted. Thus it has been observed that persons without natural ability have, through the earnestness of their devotional habits, acquired, in time, powers of sustained thought, and an accuracy and delicacy of intellectual touch, which would not else have belonged to them. The intellect being the instrument by which the soul handles religious truth, a real interest in religious truth will, of itself, often furnish an educational discipline: it alone educates an intellect which would otherwise be uneducated.[1] The moral effects of devotion are naturally more striking and abundant. Habitual prayer constantly confers decision on the wavering, and energy on the listless, and calmness on the excitable, and disinterestedness on the selfish. It braces the moral nature by transporting it into a clear, invigorating, unearthly atmosphere: it builds up the moral life, insensibly but surely remedying its deficiencies, and strengthening its weak points, till there emerges a comparatively symmetrical and consistent whole, the excellence of which all must admit, though its secret is known only to those who know it by experience.[2] Akin to the moral are the social effects of prayer. Prayer makes men, as members of society, different in their whole bearing from those who do not pray. It gilds social intercourse and conduct with a tenderness, an unobtrusiveness, a sincerity, a frankness, an evenness of

[1] Ps. cxix. 100. [2] Ps. xxvii. 4, 5, 6.

temper, a cheerfulness, a collectedness, a constant consideration for others, united to a simple loyalty to truth and duty, which leavens and strengthens society. Nay, it is not too much to say that prayer has even physical results. The countenance of a Fra Angelico reflects his spirit no less than does his art: the bright eye, the pure elevated expression, speak for themselves. It was said of one who has died within the present generation,[1] that, in his later years, his face was like that of an illuminated clock: the color and gilding had long faded away from the hands and figures; but the ravages of time were more than compensated for by the light which shone from within. This was what might have been expected in an aged man of great piety. To have lived in spirit on Mount Tabor during the years of a long life is to have caught in its closing hours some rays of the glory of the transfiguration.

Secondly, prayer is not only — perhaps, in some of the holiest souls, it is not even chiefly — a petition for something that we want, and do not possess. In the larger sense of the word, as the spiritual language of the soul, prayer is intercourse with God, often seeking no end beyond the pleasure of such intercourse. It is praise; it is congratulation; it is adoration of the infinite Majesty; it is a colloquy in which the soul engages with the All-wise and the All-holy; it is a basking in the sunshine, varied by ejaculations of thankfulness to the Sun of righteousness

[1] Rev. J. Keble.

for his light and his warmth. In this larger sense, the earlier part of the Te Deum is prayer, as much as the latter part; the earliest and latest clauses of the Gloria in Excelsis, as truly as the central ones; the Sanctus or the Jubilate, no less than the Litany; the Magnificat, as certainly as the Fifty-first Psalm. When we seek the company of our friends, we do not seek it simply with the view of getting something from them: it is a pleasure to be with them, to be talking to them at all, or about any thing; to be in possession of their sympathies, and to be showing our delight at it; to be assuring them of their place in our hearts and thoughts. So it is with the soul, when dealing with the Friend of friends,—with God. Prayer is not, as it has been scornfully described, "only a machine warranted by theologians to make God do what his clients want." It is a great deal more than petition, which is only one department of it: it is nothing less than the whole spiritual action of the soul turned towards God as its true and adequate object. And, if used in this comprehensive sense, it is clear, that as to much prayer, in the sense of spiritual intercourse with God, the question, Whether it is answered can never arise, for the simple reason that no answer is asked for.

But whether prayer means only, as in popular language it does generally mean, petition for a specific object, or the whole cycle of possible communion between the soul and God, the question, Whether it is heard is a very practical one. We do not address inanimate objects, however beautiful they may be, except in the way of poetical apostrophe. We do not enter into spiritual colloquy with the mountains, or the rivers, or the skies, with a view to discharging a duty to them, or really improving ourselves.[1] If there is really no Being above who does hear us, what can be the use of continuing a practice that is based upon an altogether false presumption? The subjective benefits of prayer depend upon our belief in its real power. But, even if they did not, who would go through a confessedly fictitious exercise, at regular intervals, with a view to securing them? Who would continue to pray regularly, if he were once well persuaded that the effect of prayer is, after all, only like the effect of the higher philosophy or poetry, — an education and a stimulus to the soul of man, but not an influence that can really touch the mind or will of that Being to whom it is addressed? Nobody denies the moral and mental stimulus which is to be gained from the study of the great poets. But do we read Homer, or Shakespeare, or Goethe, each morning and evening, and perhaps at the middle of the day? Or, if such were the practice of any of us, should we have any approach to a feeling of being guilty of a criminal omission, if, now and then, we omitted to read them? No: if prayer is to be persevered in, it must be on the strength of a conviction

[1] The apostrophes of the Psalms and the Benedicite are really acts of praise to God, of which his creatures furnish the occasion.

that it is actually heard by a living person. We cannot practise any intricate trickery upon ourselves with a view to our moral edification. We cannot pray, if we believe in our hearts that in prayer we are only holding communion with an ideal world of our own creation; that we are like children with overheated imaginations, vainly endeavoring to pass the barriers which really confine us to our dark, earthly prison-house, while, in our failure, we half consciously, half unconsciously, cheat ourselves with the consolation of talking to shapes of power or benevolence, traced by our fathers or by ourselves upon its inexorable walls. We cannot fall into the ranks of the Christian Church, lifting up the holy hands of sacrifice and intercession on all the mountains of the world, if, in our hearts, we see in her only a new company of Baal-worshippers, gathering upon the slopes of some modern Carmel, and vainly endeavoring to rouse her idol into an impossible animation, while the Elijahs of materialistic science stand by to mock her fruitless efforts with the playful scorn of that tranquil irony to which their higher knowledge presumably entitles them.

The question whether God hears prayer, is, at bottom, the question whether he is really alive; whether, in any true sense of the term, he exists at all. No word is used more equivocally than the word "God" in the present day. If by "God" we mean only a product of the thought or consciousness of man, to which it cannot be certainly presumed that any being actually corresponds; the highest thought of man, yet only man's highest thought, — then there is, of course, no one who can hear us. It has been said, that if a man talks out loud to himself, apostrophizing what are, in truth, only his own conceptions, it is difficult not to credit him with a certain tinge of madness; and it would be just as practical to address our prayer to the carved and gilded idols of Babylon, whose manufacture roused the sternest satire of the evangelical prophet, as to the unreal abstractions, which, labelled with the most holy Name, are sent us from the intellectual workshops, ancient and modern, of Alexandria or of Berlin. And if by "God" is meant only the unseen force of the universe, or its collective forces, if he is the principle of growth in the plant, the life-principle in the animal or in man, we need not read Spinoza in order to convince ourselves of the fruitlessness of prayer. A self-existing force or cause, if such can be conceived, without intelligence, without personality, of course without any moral attributes, may be a thing to wonder at; but it certainly is not a being to speak to. We may, of course, ejaculate to such a thing, if we like; but we might just as well say litanies to the winds or to the ocean. The question may be safely left to our utilitarian instincts. Time and strength, after all, are limited; and we shall not, in the long-run, spend "our money," at least in this direction, "for that which is not bread, or our labor for that which satisfieth not."[1]

[1] Isa. lv. 2.

If, on the other hand, God exists, whether we think about him or not; if he be not merely the mightiest force, the first of causes, but something more; if he be a personal being, thinking, with no limits to his thought, and willing, with no fetters around his liberty, — then, surely, we may reach him if we will. What is to prevent it? Cannot we men, at our pleasure, embody our thought, our feeling, our desires, or purposes, in language, and so make them pass into and be apprehended by the created finite personalities around us? Where is the barrier that shall arrest thought, longings, desires, entreaties, not as yet clothed (why need they be clothed?) in speech, as they mount up from the soul towards the all-embracing intelligence of God? And if God be not merely an infinite Intelligence, but a moral Being, a mighty Heart, so that justice and mercy and tenderness are attributes of his character, then to appeal to him in virtue of these attributes is assuredly to appeal to him to some purpose. If an omnipresent Intelligence is a sufficient guaranty of his being able to hear us, an interest such as justice and mercy imply on his part towards creatures who depend upon him for the original gift, and for the continued maintenance, of life, is a guaranty of his willingness to do so.

It is on this ground that God is said to hear prayer in Holy Scripture. That he should do so follows from the reality of his nature as God. Elijah's irony implies that he is unlike the Phœnician Baal in being really alive.[1] A

[1] 1 Kings xviii. 27.

later psalmist contrasts him, in like manner, with the Assyrian idols, in that "they have eyes, but see not: they have ears, but hear not."[1] They do but fill their temples with gorgeous impotence. But Israel's God is the Author of the very senses whereby we are conscious of each other's presence and wishes, and can enter into a companionship of thought and purpose. Is he debarred from the use of the gifts which he himself bestows with so bountiful a hand? "He that planted the ear, shall he not hear? or he that formed the eye, shall he not see?"[2] Is it not, on the contrary, reasonable to believe that these powers must exist in a much higher and more perfect form in the one Being who gives them than in the myriads upon whom they are bestowed, and by whom they are only held in trust? And if it is improbable, that, amid the innumerable beings who are alive to the sights and sounds of his creation, the Creator alone should be blind and deaf, is it more probable that He who has implanted in our breasts feelings of interest and pity for one another should be himself insensible to our pain and need? Our hearts must anticipate and echo the statement of the Psalmist, that God does hear the desire of the poor; that the innocent, the oppressed, the suffering, have especial claims upon him. And, to omit other illustrations, our Lord reveals him as a Father, the common Parent of men, of whose boundless love all earthly fatherhood is a shadow and a delegation.

[1] Ps. cxv. 5. [2] Ps. xciv. 9.

If the earthly parent, being evil, does not yet give a stone when his child cries for bread, the heavenly Father will not fall short of the teachings of an instinct which he has himself implanted, by failing to give the Holy Spirit to them that ask him.[1]

3.

If a man is a good Theist, we need not say a good Christian, he must believe that the Father of spirits is not deaf to the voice of the human soul; that the thanksgiving and praise, the intercessions and supplications, the penitence and the self-surrender, of beings to whom he has given moral and intellectual life, is not utterly lost upon the Giver. But will he indeed answer prayer when prayer takes the form of a petition for some specific blessing which must be either granted or refused? There is no doubt as to the reply which the Bible and the Church have given to this question. But what do some modern thinkers say about it? Do they not deny the power of prayer by surrounding the throne of God with barriers, which, as they would have it, oblige him, while "the sorrowful sighings of the prisoners" of this vale of tears incessantly "come before him," to make as though he heard not, and to shorten his hand as if it could not save?

The first presumed barrier against the efficacy of prayer,

[1] Luke xi. 11–13.

to which men point, is the scientific idea of law, reigning throughout the spiritual as well as the material universe. This idea, as we are constantly reminded, is one of the most remarkable conquests of modern thought; and no man, so it is said, can enter into it with an intelligent sympathy, without abandoning the fond conceit that God will grant a particular favor to one of his creatures upon being asked to do so. It may have been pardonable to pray for rain, for health, for freedom from pestilence and famine, when these things were supposed to depend upon the caprice of an omnipotent Will; but the scientific idea of law renders these prayers absurd. We know that a shower is the product of atmospheric laws which make a shower, under certain circumstances, inevitable; that the death of an individual is the result of physiological laws which absolutely determine it. The idea that a shower, or the death of a man, is contingent upon the good pleasure of a Being who can avert or precipitate them at pleasure is unscientific: it belongs to days when the idea of law had not yet dawned upon the intellect of civilization, or when, at any rate, large margins of the physical world, and the whole of the spiritual world, were supposed to be beyond its frontiers, as being abandoned to the government of a capricious Omnipotence. Surely, it is added, we have really attained to a nobler idea of the universe than was this old theological conception of the Bible and the Church: the superiority is to be measured by those fundamental instincts of fitness within us, which assign to law and order a higher place in our minds than can belong to a personal will.

Does not the very word "law," by reason of its majestic and imposing associations, here involve us in some indistinctness of thought? What do we mean by law? When we speak of a law of Nature, are we thinking of some self-sustained, invisible force, of which we can give no account, except that here it is, a matter of experience? Or do we mean by a law of Nature only a principle, which, as our observation shows us, appears to govern particular actions of the almighty Agent who made, and who upholds, the universe? If the former, let us frankly admit that we have not merely fettered God's freedom: we have, alas! ceased to believe in him. For such self-sustained force is either self-originating (in which case there is no being in existence who has made all that constitutes this universe); or otherwise, having derived its first impact from the creative will of God, this force has subsequently escaped altogether from his control, so that it now fetters his liberty; and, in this case, there is no being in existence who is almighty in the sense of being really master of this universe. If, however, we mean by law the observed regularity with which God works in nature as in grace, then, in our contact with law, we are dealing, not with a brutal, unintelligent, unconquerable force, but with the free-will of an intelligent and moral Artist, who works, in his perfect freedom, with sustained and beautiful symmetry. Where is the absurdity of asking him to hold his hand, or to hasten his work? He to whom we pray may be trusted to grant or to refuse a prayer, as may seem best to the highest wisdom and the truest love. And, if he grant it, he is not without resources, even although we should have asked him to suspend what we call a natural law. Can he not, then, provide for the freedom of his action without violating its order? Can he not supersede a lower rule of working by the intervention of a higher? If he really works at all, if something that is neither moral nor intelligent has not usurped his throne, it is certain that "the thing that is done upon earth he doeth it himself;" and that it is, therefore, as consistent with reason as with reverence to treat him as being a free Agent, who is not really tied and bound by the intellectual abstractions with which finite intellects would fain annihilate the freedom of his action.

No: to pray for rain or sunshine, for health or food, is just as reasonable as to pray for gifts which the soul only can receive, — increased love, joy, peace, long-suffering, gentleness, goodness, faith. All such prayers presuppose the truth, that God is not the slave of his own rules of action; that he can innovate upon his work without forfeiting his perfection; that law is only our way of conceiving of his regularized working, and not an external force, which governs and moulds what we recognize as his work. It dissolves into thin air as we look hard at it, this fancied barrier of inexorable law; and, as the mist clears off, beyond there is the throne of the moral King of the universe, in whose eyes material symmetry is as nothing when compared with the spiritual well-being of his moral creatures.

A second barrier to the efficacy of prayer is sometimes discovered in the truth, that all which comes to pass is fore-determined in the predestination of God. "How is the efficacy of prayer to be reconciled," asks the fatalistic pre-destinarian, "with the boundless power and knowledge of God?" Is not every thing that happens to us the decision of an almighty, wise, beneficent Will, — a Will which, in human phrase, has ordained it from all eternity? Could this Will have been, could it be, other than it is? Has time any meaning for it? Is it not, in its omniscience and omnipotence, eternally what it is? Where, then, is there any room for the effect of prayer? Can it be conceived that the erring understanding and finite will of the creature will be allowed to impose its decisions on the infallible mind and resistless determinations of God? Surely if we are to go on praying, after recognizing the sovereignty of God, we must give up the notion of exerting a real influence upon the divine Will: we must content ourselves with resignation, with bringing our minds into conformity with that which, as a matter of fact, is quite beyond the range of our influence.

This language does but carry us into one department of the old controversy between the defenders of the sovereignty of God on the one side, and the advocates of the free-will of man on the other. The very idea of God as it occurs to the human mind, and the distinct statements of revelation, alike represent the divine Will as exerting sovereign and resistless sway. If it were otherwise, God would not be almighty; that is, he would not be God. On the other hand, our daily experience, and the language of Scripture, both assure us that man is literally a free agent: his freedom is the very ground of his moral and religious responsibility. Are these two truths hopelessly incompatible with each other? So it may seem at first sight; and if we escape the danger of denying the one in the supposed interests of the other, if we shrink from sacrificing God's sovereignty to man's free-will with Arminius, and from sacrificing man's freedom to God's sovereignty with Calvin, we can only express a wise ignorance by saying, that to us they seem like parallel lines, which must meet at a point in eternity far beyond our present range of view. We do know, however, that, being both true, they cannot really contradict each other; and that, in some manner which we cannot formulate, the divine sovereignty must not merely be compatible with, but must even imply, the perfect freedom of created wills. So it is with prayer and the divine predestination. God orders all that happens to us, and, in virtue of his infinite knowledge, by eternal decrees. But he also says to us, in the plainest language, that he does answer prayer, and that practically his dealings with us are governed, in matters of the greatest importance, as well as of the least, by the petitions which we address to him. What if prayers and actions to us at the moment perfectly spontaneous are eternally foreseen, and included within the all-embracing predestination of God, as factors and causes, working out that final result, which, beyond all dispute, is the product of his good pleasure? Whether I open my mouth, or lift my hand, is, before my doing it, strictly within the jurisdiction and power of my personal will; but, however I may decide, my decision, so absolutely free to me, will have been already incorporated by the all-seeing, all-controlling Being, as an integral part, however insignificant, of his one, all-embracing purpose, leading on to effects and causes beyond itself. Prayer, too, is only a foreseen action of man, which, together with its results, is embraced in the eternal predestination of God. To us, this or that blessing may be strictly contingent on our praying for it; but our prayer is, nevertheless, so far from necessarily introducing change into the purpose of the unchangeable, that it has been all along taken, so to speak, into account by him. If, then, with "the Father of lights" there is, in this sense, "no variableness, neither shadow of turning," it is not, therefore, irrational to pray for specific blessings, as we do in the Litany, because God works out his plans not merely in us, but by us; and we may dare to say that that which is to us a free self-determination may be not other than a foreseen element of his work.

A third barrier supposed to interfere with the efficacy of

prayer is the false idea of the divine dignity, which is borrowed from our notions of human royalties. It is assumed that a supreme governor cannot be expected to take account of trifling circumstances, or to decide between petty and conflicting claims. He legislates for the universe; but it is not to be supposed that he will also discharge all the minute and harassing duties of a local executive. The power of prayer implies a special providence; and a special providence, we are told, is beneath the dignity of God. We have already encountered this line of thought, not in its practical bearings upon prayer, but as it affects our belief as to the divine nature. "Do you imagine," men ask, "when you reflect upon the vast universe in which we live, upon that immeasurable space, upon those innumerable worlds, upon those systems beyond systems of suns which are discovering themselves slowly but surely to our telescopes, that He who made this mighty whole has nothing to do but to listen to the little story of your wants and hopes and fears? He has instituted some good and universal rules of government under which you live: if they sometimes bear hardly upon you, your case is only that of others, and you must take your chance. To expect him to suspend, or to revoke, his legislation on your particular account, is to sacrifice common sense to outrageous egotism, — the egotism which can suppose that a petty individual life, a worm crawling on the surface of one of his smallest planets, can be an object of this particular consideration and interest to the almighty Creator."

Even at the risk of representing human egotism, it must be here and again asserted, that man's place in the creation is not determined by the considerations which this objection supposes. In the eyes of an intellectual and spiritual being, material bulk is not the only or the highest test of greatness. If God is not to be supposed to be mainly interested in vast accumulations of senseless matter; if there be, in the estimate of a moral being, other and worthier measures of greatness; if the organic be higher than the inorganic, and that which feels, than that which has no feeling; if that which thinks be higher than that which only feels, and that which freely conforms to moral will higher than that which only thinks; if a fly be really a nobler thing than a granite mountain, and a little child than a rhinoceros or a mammoth, — then we need not acquiesce in this depreciatory estimate of man's place in creation, or of his claims upon the ear of God. On his bodily side, man is insignificant enough. As a spirit concious of his own existence, and determining his action in the freedom of his will, he does not deceive himself in believing that God has crowned him with an especial glory and honor among the visible creatures.[1] But, even if man were not thus honored, it is, as we have seen, no part of the divine dignity to be inattentive even to the lowest creatures of his hand. The throne of heaven is not modelled upon the type of an Oriental depotism; and God's greatness is not

[1] Ps. viii. 5.

compromised by the duties of administration any more than it is heightened by the enactment of law. The infinite Mind is not less capable of formulating the most universal principles, because he enters with perfect sympathy and intelligence into each of our separate wants and efforts,—the wants and efforts of creatures who are really greater, because infinitely more like, their Creator, than are the largest stars and suns.

A fourth barrier to the efficacy of prayer is supposed to be discoverable in an inadequate conception of the interests of human beings as a whole. To suppose that God can answer individual prayers for specific blessings is inconsistent, we are told, with any serious appreciation of human interests. One man or nation asks for that which may be an injury to another. The Spaniards prayed for the success of their Armada: the English prayed against it. Both could not be listened to. The weather cannot consult the convenience of everybody at once: and therefore the specific prayers of well-meaning villagers, if they could be attended to, could only be attended to by a God, who, instead of being the Father of all his creatures, reserved special indulgences for his favorites.

Here it is natural to remark, that, if God should think fit to grant a large proportion of the particular requests which would be found among the daily prayers of an earnest Christian, he would not, to say the least, thereby do any injury to others, whether they were Christians or not.

Prayer for the highest well-being of any human being may be granted without damaging other human beings. If God should condescend, in answer to prayer, to teach one of his servants more humility, purity, or love, this would not oblige him to withdraw spiritual graces from any others in order to do it. Nor are other persons the worse for coming into contact with one whom God has made loving, or pure, or humble, in answer to prayer. Is it not nearer the truth to say that they are likely to be much better; and, therefore, that a large number of answers to prayer for personal blessings necessarily extend, in their effects, beyond those who are immediately blessed?

But observe, further, that every prayer for specific blessings in a Christian soul is tacitly, if not expressly, conditioned. The three conditions which are always understood are given at the beginning of the Lord's Prayer, — "Hallowed be thy name, thy kingdom come, thy will be done." In effect, these three conditions are only one. If a change of weather, or a restoration to health, or any blessing, be prayed for, a Christian petitioner deliberately wills that his prayer should be refused, supposing that to grant it should in any way obscure God's glory in other minds, or hinder the advance of his kingdom, and so contravene what must be his will. Every Christian tacitly adds to every prayer, "Nevertheless, not my will, but thine, be done." All Christian prayer takes it for granted, first, that the material world exists for the sake of, and is entirely subordinate to, the interests of the moral; and, secondly, that God is the best judge of what the true interests of the moral world really are. Therefore, if his specific petition is not granted, a Christian will not conclude that his real prayer is unanswered. His real prayer was, from the first, that God's name might be hallowed among men by the advance of his kingdom and the doing of his will, through God's granting a particular request which he urges. He knows that his own highest object may be best secured by the refusal of the very blessing for which he pleads; and he puts his finite knowledge and his narrow sympathies into the hands of infinite Wisdom and infinite Love, with perfect confidence that the final decision will be the best answer to his real and deepest prayer. It is thus that he realizes the promise, "Every one that asketh receiveth." He, too, receives that which he really wants, though his specific petition should be refused.

A last barrier to faith in the efficacy of prayer is really to be discovered in man's idea of his own self-sufficiency. It can scarcely be doubted that one of the excellences of our character as a nation is constantly a source of danger to our faith in the power of prayer. Pelagius was himself a native of Britain; and the old heresy of substituting human self-sufficiency for dependence on the grace and help of God is very congenial to the temper which we English cultivate, with such success, in individual action and in political life. After all, we say, do we not depend on our

20

own efforts for being what we are, and for doing what we do? Whatever God may see fit to do for us, our best form of prayer is work: it is the determination to secure what we want by personal efforts to get it. The indolent or the imaginative may be left to lengthen out their litanies; but practical men will fall back upon the wise proverb, that "God helps those who help themselves."

Here, however, it must be insisted on by the one side, and admitted on the other, that many objects of prayer are altogether out of the reach of human effort, and that, if they are to be secured at all, they must be given freely by God. But the fact of our moral freedom, as felt in the capacity for work, to which Pelagianism appeals, is not more clear than the fact of our dependence. Do what we will, we depend on others: we are linked to them by a thousand ties. We are, all of us, acted upon most powerfully by the circumstances which surround us: the governing moods of thought and feeling within ourselves are often determined by these circumstances. This is true of "self-made men," as we call them, not less than of others. How much did not Faraday owe to Sir Humphry Davy! And this dependence upon circumstances is, in fact, dependence upon things which God controls. Facts are not less facts because they seem to be incompatible, because the effort to reconcile them teaches our reason that its limits are narrower than we wish. It is easier to say that man is entirely free, that he depends on nothing, or to say that man is simply the creature of circumstances, that he is never really free, than to say, what is the real truth, that man is, in his entire freedom, absolutely dependent, that he is, in his entire dependence, absolutely free. Yet this apparent paradox is the literal truth, which refuses to ignore facts in order to make the task of reason easier, and to enable it the better to round off its trenchant but inconclusive theories about human action. And, because life is so subtle an intermixture of dependence and action, prayer is the most practical of all forms of work: it is at once the activity of man's freedom, and the expression of his dependence; and the answer which it wins is not less, in one sense, the result of human effort, than, in another, it is the work of God.

And thus it is in and by prayer that the two governing elements of religious life, thought and work, alike find their strongest impulse and their point of unity. Such is our weakness, that we constantly tend to a one-sided use of God's gifts. We are either absorbingly speculative and contemplative on the one hand, or we are absorbingly practical, and men of action, on the other. Either exaggeration is fatal to the true life of religion, which binds the soul to God by faith as well as by love, by love not less than by faith, by a life of energetic service not less truly than by a life of communion with light and truth. It is in prayer that each element is at once quickened in itself, and balanced by the presence of the other. The great masters and teachers of Christian doctrine have always found in prayer their highest source of illumination. Not to go beyond the limits of the English Church, it is recorded of Bishop Andrewes, that he spent five hours daily on his knees. The greatest practical resolves that have enriched and beautified human life in Christian times have been arrived at in prayer, ever since the day when, at the most solemn service of the apostolical Church, the Holy Ghost said, "Separate me Barnabas and Saul for the work whereunto I have called them."[1] It is prayer which prevents religion from degenerating into mere religious thought on the one side, or into mere philanthropy on the other. In prayer, the man of action will never become so absorbed in his work as to be indifferent to the truth which is its original motive. In prayer, the man of study and contemplation will never forget that truth is given, not so much that it may interest and stimulate our understandings, as that it may govern and regenerate our life. And thus it is, that prayer is of such vital importance to the well-being of the soul. Study may be dispensed with by those who work with their hands for God; handiwork may be dispensed with by those who seek him in books and in thought: but prayer is indispensable, alike for workers and students, alike for scholar and peasant, alike for the educated and the unlettered; for we all have to seek God's face above: we all have souls to be sanctified and saved; we all have sins and passions to beat back and to conquer. And these things are achieved pre-

1 Acts xiii. 2.

eminently by prayer, which is properly and representatively the action of religion. It is the action whereby we men, in all our frailty and defilement, associate ourselves with our divine Advocate on high, and realize the sublime bond which in him, the one Mediator between God and man, unites us in our utter unworthiness to the strong and all-holy God.

That prayer, sooner or later, is answered, to all who have prayed earnestly and constantly, is, in different degrees, a matter of personal experience. David, Elijah, Hezekiah, Daniel, the apostles of Christ, were not the victims of an illusion, in virtue of which they connected particular events which would have happened in any case with prayers that preceded it. They who never pray, or who never pray with the humility, confidence, and importunity that wins its way to the heart of God, cannot speak from experience as to the effects of prayer; nor are they in a position to give credit, with generous simplicity, to those who can. But at least, on such a subject as this, the voice of the whole company of God's servants may be held to counterbalance a few *à priori* surmises or doctrines; and it is the very heart of humanity itself, which, from age to age, mounts up with the Psalmist to the eternal throne, "O thou that hearest prayer, unto thee shall all flesh come."[1] And Christians can penetrate within the veil. They know that there is a majestic pleading, which for eighteen centuries has never ceased, and which is

[1] Ps. lxv. 2.

itself omnipotent,—the pleading of One who makes their cause his own. They rest upon the divine words, "Whatsoever ye shall ask the Father, in my name, he will give it you."[1]

A time will probably come to most of us, if it has not come to some already, when we shall wish that the hours at our command, during the short day of life, had not been disposed of as they have. After all, this world is a poor thing to live for, when the next is in view. Whatever be their claims, created beings have no business to be sitting on that highest throne within the soul that belongs to the Creator. Yet, for all that, too often they do sit there. And time is passing. Of that priceless gift of time, how much will one day be seen to have been lost! how ruinous shall we deem our investment of this our most precious stock! How many interests, occupations, engagements, friendships,—I speak not of the avowed ways of "killing time," as it is termed with piteous accuracy,—will be then regarded only as so many precautions for building our house upon the sand, as only so many expedients for assuring our failure to compass the true end of our existence! It may not now seem possible that we should ever think thus. Life is like the summer's day; and in the first fresh morning we do not realize the noonday heat; and at noon we do not think of the shadows lengthening across the plain, and of the setting sun, and of the advancing night. Yet to each

[1] John xvi. 23.

and all the sunset comes at last; and those who have made most of the day are not unlikely to reflect most bitterly how little they have made of it. Whatever else they may look back upon with thankfulness or with sorrow, it is certain that they will regret no omissions of duty more keenly than neglect of prayer; that they will prize no hours more than those which have been passed, whether in private or in public, before that throne of justice and of grace upon which they hope to gaze throughout eternity.

www.ingramcontent.com/pod-product-compliance
Lightning Source LLC
LaVergne TN
LVHW020236110826
845151LV00003B/940

* 9 7 8 1 4 2 5 5 3 0 7 5 4 *